INTERNATIONAL LAW
IN
A CHANGING WORLD

C. Wilfred Jenks   Jimenez de Arechaga   Radhabinod Pal
Roberto Ago   Arthur H. Dean   T. O. Elias
Oscar Schacter   Grigori I. Tunkin   Leslie Munro
Andre Gros   Paul Guggenheim   Jean S. Pictet
　　　　　　　　　　Dag Hammarskjold

Published in Cooperation
with the United Nations

1963

Oceana Publications, Inc.

Dobbs Ferry, New York

© Copyright, 1963, by Oceana Publications, Inc.

Library of Congress Catalog Card Number 63-13581

Manufactured in the United States of America

TABLE OF CONTENTS

I	Law, Freedom and Welfare in Action for Peace by C. Wilfred Jenks (I.L.O.)	1
II	The State and International Organisation by Professor Roberto Ago (Italy)	12
III	Liberty and Law in International Life by Dag Hammarskjöld (United Nations)	22
IV	Dag Hammarskjöld and the Relation of Law to Politics by Oscar Schachter (United Nations)	33
V	Peaceful Settlement of International Disputes Mediation and Conciliation by Professor Andre Gros (France)	44
VI	The International Court of Justice and the Judicial Settlement of International Disputes by Professor Jimenez de Aréchaga (Uruguay)	54
VII	The Importance of International Law in the Maintenance of Peace by Arthur H. Dean (USA)	64
VIII	International Law and Peace by Professor Grigori I. Tunkin (USSR)	72
IX	The Birth of Autonomous International Law by Professor Paul Guggenheim (Switzerland)	80
X	International Law in a Changing World by Professor Radhabinod Pal (India)	88
XI	The Expanding Frontiers of Public International Law by Dr. T. O. Elias	97
XII	Law and Outer Space by Sir Leslie Munro (New Zealand)	105
XIII	The Development of International Humanitarian Law by Jean S. Pictet (Switzerland)	114

FOREWORD

Little is generally known, outside specialist circles, about the development of international law and its relation to the growing number of those international organizations which have become essential features of our modern society.

In this book world-famous experts in the field of international law present their views on a subject of importance to everyone interested in the development of international relations.

Many of the contributions are based on the texts of a series of lectures given by eminent jurists under the auspices of the European Office of the United Nations and the International Lawyers Club in Geneva.

This publication has been prepared by the Oceana Publications, Inc. in cooperation with the United Nations.

        OFFICE OF PUBLIC INFORMATION
        UNITED NATIONS

INTRODUCTION

In 1914, there were only 55 independent States in the world. Today, there are over 100. What changes, if any, have occurred in their legal relationships with one another? Are the mutual dealings of States, as we see them in the United Nations and other international bodies, different in any way from what they were?

In the past, the two main duties of States were the maintenance of internal order and external security. Nationalism and sovereignty were the concepts on which international law rested, and the idea of one nation having duties towards the citizens of an independent, foreign country was not entertained by statesmen. Broadly speaking, international law reflected the principles by which the Western powers agreed to live and to conduct their business in the 18th and 19th centuries. It aimed at the peaceful settlement of disputes between those powers and at the protection of their national sovereignty.

The great changes witnessed in our century have brought new elements into this picture. On the one hand, many governments have assumed various degrees of responsibility for the welfare of their own citizens, in ways undreamed of a hundred years ago. On the other, a trend has set in by which countries are beginning to accept a certain responsibility for the well-being and advancement of other peoples than their own. Technical assistance and the diverse forms of international aid are an illustration of that tendency.

Side by side with this more positive approach to the duties of States has gone a certain abandonment by them of the complete independence from outside control which was formerly an axiom of government policy. Evidence of this is to be seen in the numerous conventions ratified by the Member States of the United Nations family of organizations, each requiring policies or action decided upon by international agreement. In smaller regional groupings, such as common markets and free-trade areas, a similar tendency is visible towards the international alignment of policy, involving changes in national legislation and practice to satisfy the common interest of the group.

There was perhaps never a time when the need for a generally accepted system of international law was so pressing as it is today. Traditional international law is being subjected to increasing scrutiny and the non-specialists will want some light on fundamental questions.

What is international law? How far can it offer a stabilizing influence in a time of violence? What are some of the items on its balance sheet of achievement and failure? Does it satisfy the 100 nations, as it did the 55? How could it be made more effective?

These are questions which concern us all. They are vital at a time when so many new nations are readjusting their relationships to the rest of the world and when the skies may become at any moment a pathway for long-range weapons of destruction.

To help in finding answers to such questions, the United Nations Information Service in Geneva and the International Lawyers Club (Geneva) arranged a series of lectures by eminent jurists from various countries, each of whom enjoys an international reputation.

The following texts are based on those lectures. They have been somewhat shortened in order to make them more suitable for the many students of world problems who are interested in the maintenance of peace, but who do not possess specialized legal knowledge.

In addition, a contribution has been obtained from an eminent African lawyer on the new African states and the relevance of international law to their needs. The volume also contains the text of an address on "Liberty and Law in International Life" which was given in Philadelphia in 1955 by the late Secretary-General of the United Nations, Dag Hammarskjold, and an essay on "Dag Hammarskjold and the Relation of Law to Politics" by Oscar Schachter, Director in the Office of Legal Affairs of the United Nations, reprinted from the *American Journal of International Law*.

Law, Freedom and Welfare in Action For Peace
by C. Wilfed Jenks

C. Wilfred Jenks: b. 1909. 1948: Assistant Director-General, International Labour Office; 1940: Legal Adviser, ILO; Representative of ILO at Bretton Woods, San Francisco and numerous other international conferences, including UN General Assembly and Economic and Social Council; Vice-President, Second International Congress of Labour Law; 1931: entered Legal Section, ILO.

"The State comes into existence to satisfy the bare needs of life, it continues in existence to make life good." Aristotle's evaluation, though made in the fourth century B.C., remains an apt comment on the contemporary development of international organization.

Historically, international law and international organization are a product of the revulsion against war. That revulsion sought a remedy for the evils of war in either political action or legal procedures.

In its earlier phases the political movement towards international organization was an essentially European attempt, in a world dominated by the independence of States, to revive the concept of a universal polity which had dominated the thought of the Middle Ages. Twice during the nineteenth century, in its first quarter and its last, the Concert of Europe appeared about to become a reality, but its geographical base was too narrow and the divergence of interests and outlook proved too profound.

The legal approach developed more slowly. Despite a beginning under the Jay Treaty of 1795, and the success of the Alabama Arbitration in 1872, it was not until the Hague peace conferences of 1899 and 1907 that the subject became a serious preoccupation of statesmen. When the test came in 1914, neither the political nor the legal approach had produced anything sufficiently solid to maintain the peace.

Premonitions of a New Approach

Meanwhile, economic and technological developments were creating new needs for international co-operation. The creation of the International Telegraph Union in 1865, the Universal Postal Union in 1874 and the International Meteorological Organization in 1878, were premonitions of a new approach. By 1914 the antecedents of eight of the present specialized agencies of the United Nations began to be clearly discernible. In only two of the fields now catered for by major United Nations agencies, that of education, science and culture (except as regards copyright) and that of atomic energy, does the story of international action not date back before 1914.

Statesmen and lawyers had little to do with these new tendencies. Foreign offices and treasuries tolerated, rather than encouraged, them. The sovereignty of States was therefore not the dominant principle in discussing the type of organization and procedures required. Important innovations were thus introduced unchallenged and were not regarded at the time as having any bearing on the future of international politics. Ignored by the great ones of the world and the international lawyers, these developments were irrelevant to the catastrophe of 1914, and this fact helped them to survive it. They assumed a new significance in the revaluation of the problem of international organization which resulted from it, and which led to the birth of the League of Nations and of the International Labour Office (ILO). It was Leonard Woolf who in 1916 first drew widespread attention to the potentialities of the existing organizations, and his writings greatly influenced the thinking of Edward Phelan, to whom the world owes the most original and successful outcome of international thinking at that time, the Constitution of the ILO.

Concepts of 1920

On the political side, the Covenant of the League of Nations expressed ethical values which were rather an inheritance from the nineteenth century than a philosophy for the new age produced by world war, revolution, and accelerated economic and social change. The League of Nations ultimately failed because it lacked any real grip on the common imagination and because statesmen shrank from the risks of making it succeed. The ordinary citizen did not feel that his personal freedom and welfare were at stake in Manchuria, in Ethiopia or in the Rhineland.

Other voices, however, were being lifted in favour of a broader concept of international organization. Among these were those of Jan Smuts, Arthur Salter and Albert Thomas.

In December 1918 Smuts already foresaw needs and processes which the United Nations system is now only beginning to recognize and devise. "My reflections", he wrote, "have convinced me that the ordinary conception of the League of Nations is not a fruitful one, nor is it the right one, and that a radical transformation of it is necessary. If the League is ever to be a success, it will have to occupy a much greater position and perform many other functions besides those ordinarily assigned to it. Peace and war are resultants of many complex forces, and those forces will have to be gripped at an earlier stage of their growth, if peace is to be effectively maintained. To enable it to do so the League will have to occupy the great position which has been rendered vacant by the destruction of so many of the old European empires." Smuts, however, still thought of the League as a predominantly European instrument. He could not have foreseen how great would be the vacuum created by the passing away of the old European order.

Salter added an economic dimension to the Wilsonian philosophy. He sought to promote international discussion of economic issues before national policy became irrevocable. Unhappily, looking back to 1914, he saw the problem too much in terms of "recovery" or "retrieving security" rather than one of coping with the new economic consequences of a series of revolutions still in their initial phases. The impact of the great depression, the Keynesian revolution and the Second World War have transformed the economic outlook of contemporary international organization. While the League sought to restore the free economies of 1914, the United Nations was directed by the Charter to promote higher standards of living than those which obtained in 1939 and to foster conditions of economic and social progress.

Within the League of Nations system an alternative policy, symbolized by the International Labour Office, will be forever associated with the genius of Albert Thomas. His personal influence did much to substitute the wellbeing of individuals for the mutual relations of States as the primary concern of international organization, and so to set a pattern for the creation of specialized agencies, as we know them today. This concept of a world organization affirming human rights and promoting steps to guarantee them on a universal basis was altogether revolutionary.

The United Nations Charter

The Charter of the United Nations represented a provisional summing-up of these three tendencies: Smuts' idea of a world organization fulfilling functions which few modern States could discharge for themselves, Salter's concept of the interpenetration of international and national economic and financial policy and Albert Thomas' vision that the ultimate test of policy is its impact on individual human lives.

One generation has therefore seen a fundamental change in the whole concept of world organization, corresponding to a transformation of the functions and responsibilities of the State. International lawyers have not yet met the challenge thus presented to them regarding the nature and scale of their responsibilities and opportunities. Law almost always lags behind life. Despite the lasting contribution made to the development of international law during the last forty years by such great figures as Max Huber, Politis, Van Vollenhoven, Kelsen, Manley Hudson, Georges Scelle, Hersch Lauterpacht and others, the broader concept of international organization has been only partly reflected in a widening and deepening of the rule of law.

Thus, we see that governments have eschewed compulsory jurisdiction because the law is uncertain, and that the law remains uncertain because governments fight shy of compulsory jurisdiction. Without a larger measure of compulsory jurisdiction, adjudication cannot play its necessary part in developing the law as a bulwark of freedom and welfare. The tendency of some emerging States to distrust the existing law presents the most complex and challenging problem confronting international law in our time. The situation calls for a longer perspective in the attitude of the older States, which have been apt to regard international law as a projection of their own values, and for a mature acceptance by the newer States of responsibility for helping to uphold and promote the development of common legal standards which the interests of the whole world require.

One of the most encouraging features of recent years, greatly accentuated since 1950 by the United Nations Expanded Programme of Technical Assistance and the Special Fund, has been the increasing extent to which international organizations have been called upon to discharge operational responsibilities. While there has been a tendency to exaggerate in some quarters the desirability of a shift of emphasis by the international organizations from law to action, the necessary balance is now tending to be restored. In the ILO such a balance has been retained throughout for, as Mr. David Morse has pointed out with reference to the ILO, "The legislative work of the Organization, though now seen in a new perspective, has lost none of its intrinsic importance".

Against this background, what significant contribution can law make in our time to freedom and welfare?

Law and Freedom

The progress of self-government is essentially a political process but, when we pass to the protection of human rights, the potential contribution of law to freedom becomes much greater. The Universal Declaration of Human Rights, while it represents a major step towards the definition of the rights postulated by the Charter, does not purport to embody legal obligations binding on Member States. Advances on more limited fronts have, however, occurred. They include the negotiation, under the auspices of the Council of Europe, of a European Convention for the

Protection of Human Rights and Fundamental Freedoms and the establishment of a European Commission of Human Rights and a European Court of Human Rights.

On a broader international basis, the International Labour Organization has adopted a number of Conventions of which that on Forced Labour has received 78 ratifications. This piecemeal approach has made it possible for many States to undertake firm obligations relating to an important series of human rights in the social field. A series of similar Conventions dealing with such matters as freedom of opinion and expression, freedom of peaceful assembly, freedom from arbitrary arrest, detention or exile and the presumption of innocence until proof of guilt, would be a major contribution in resolving the deadlock over the proposed International Covenants on Human Rights. A bold initiative in this direction might progressively attract support. Few would have been so rash as to predict the number of ratifications which have been secured by the ILO for Conventions relating to basic human rights.

Law and Welfare

How far can the law make a similar contribution to welfare?

The invitation to deliver this lecture reached me by letter in Buenos Aires thanks to arrangements made by the Universal Postal Union. I cabled my acceptance through facilities operated in accordance with the rules of the International Telecommunication Union. I later crossed three continents by air services made possible by the rules and facilities of the International Civil Aviation Organization and the World Meteorological Organization. I was exempt from quarantine because I held a certificate of vaccination issued by the World Health Organization. Seven international organizations had some part in my being here.

Communications

The emergence of a generally accepted body of world law in such fields has already brought about a revolution in everyday life. Before the foundation of the Universal Postal Union in 1874, international postal rates were high, complex and in some respects uncertain. Today over 100 member administrations of the Universal Postal Union have agreed to uniform regulations governing every aspect of the letter post. Similarly, the international telegraph and telephone service, sound broadcasting and television, radio between ships and air navigation would be impossible without the regulations administered by the International Telecommunication Union. With the increasing use of radar and the prospect of space devices being used for telecommunications, the problems calling for international regulation become ever more complex.

Aviation

Aviation is governed by a detailed body of international rules. Without this complex of rules and of arrangements for their regular revision in the light of new technical developments, there could have been no scheduled air services. The switch over from propeller to jet propulsion and the prospect of supersonic speeds are now being reflected in a thorough reconsideration of many existing rules and practices.

Health

Aviation has emphasized the need for adequate arrangements to control the spread of disease. In this field, we have an imposing and growing body of international rules. Such regulations come into force for all member States of the World Health Organization, after due notice has been given of their adoption by the World Health Assembly, except for such States as may announce within a given period their rejection of them or specific reservations. The International Sanitary Regulations restate in one document various international sanitary laws developed from 1851 onwards. We are so preoccupied today with cancer and coronary thrombosis because the less subtle dangers of cholera, plague, smallpox, typhoid and yellow fever have been virtually eliminated by medical science with the aid of international law.

Currency and Tariffs

A generation ago, unfettered control of currency and tariffs was one of the hallmarks of sovereignty. Today such control belongs to the past for members of the International Monetary Fund, and for parties to the General Agreement on Tariffs and Trade. In early League of Nations days, tariff policy was regarded as perhaps the question of domestic jurisdiction *par excellence*. Monetary and tariff policy are now being brought within the realm of law.

Investment

In the field of investment, the International Bank has evolved a novel body of autonomous law governing its own operations. Private investment for economic development will be acceptable to developing countries only on equitable terms which respect their hard-won independence, but potential investors will require adequate guarantee against expropriation or discriminatory treatment. An international charter has been proposed to reconcile these conflicting considerations by the application of general principles.

Social Objectives

The social objectives of economic policy have now won a secure place in the law. The International Labour Code embodies detailed obligations and standards for the implementation of the objective that "All human beings, irrespective of race, creed or sex, have the right to pursue both their material wellbeing and their spiritual development in conditions of freedom and dignity, economic security and equal opportunity." The Code now comprises 116 Conventions and 115 Recommendations. Ninety-eight of these Conventions are in force and have received a total of 2,374 ratifications from 97 different countries and 1,285 acceptances in respect of 84 non-metropolitan territories. There is an elaborate system for checking the practical fulfilment of these obligations. The ILO has contributed much, and in many different ways, to the law of international organization, but nothing, perhaps, of more lasting value than these arrangements for mutual supervision of the obligations assumed by States which ratify its Conventions.

Nuclear Energy

We tend to think of scientific and technological progress in the dramatic forms in which they are posed by nuclear testing or the so-called race for the moon and stars, but the need for legal regulation covers a much wider field and embraces many subjects on which agreement may more readily be reached. The international law of nuclear energy to which the International Atomic Energy Agency and the European Nuclear Energy Agency are making a significant contribution in co-operation with specialized agencies of the United Nations and other bodies embraces such matters as safeguards against the diversion of fissile material from peaceful purposes, its safe carriage, protection from radiation, the disposal of radioactive waste, liability for damage or injury due to nuclear dangers and nuclear risk insurance.

New Categories of Thought

These broad fields represent new categories of thought for the international lawyer. How far they take us from the preoccupation of the past with such matters as territorial rights, diplomatic and consular immunities, belligerency and neutrality, or even from the more recent preoccupation with such matters as the justiciability of international disputes! Traditional law on these matters has given us the elements of a structure of the society of States on the basis of which we can consolidate the achievements of the past and evolve a common law of mankind for a world community. The view that the international lawyer's primary responsibility is less to preserve the heritage of the past than to discharge his obligations to the future was once regarded as dangerously heretical. It now commands the wholehearted assent of all that is most vital and persuasive in contemporary legal thought.

In our time, growing technological uniformity and the concentration of military power in a few hands are offset by a wider diffusion of political vitality among many States and an increasing diversity of vigorous cultures. The common law of mankind must therefore draw upon the richly varied legal traditions of all parts of the world. This approach has been criticized as unrealistic by those who claim that ideological differences are too broad and deep to be bridged by the acceptance of common legal principles, that Asian and African legal systems are so little adapted to modern needs that their contribution will be to weaken, rather than strengthen, the development of law, and that the general experience of comparative lawyers in this regard has been discouraging. Only the future can decide the controversy but, for my part, I await the verdict with confidence.

Need for Diversity of Institutions

The structure of international organization has now become so complex, and at times appears to be so much the product of historical accidents, that drastic modification of it is often suggested, but the existing decentralization of international organization reflects realities. Our problem is infinitely more complex than that of any government or any worldwide industrial concern. It is to bring into an effective world partnership all of the functions of government and all the varied economic interests involved in contemporary international relations. This requires the intermeshing of policy and action at hundreds of different points. The diversity of our existing international institutions reflects this fundamental reality.

A New Epoch in Political Thinking

Internationally, we are working our way towards a new form of functional federalism rather than towards central executive authority under a central, quasi-parliamentary control. While there must be an important degree of centralization for the discussion of general policies and the maintenance of world peace, the forces in play are too various and spontaneous to permit of an approach to international organization inconsistent with the principle of government by consent of the governed. It is impossible to transpose government institutions originally evolved for small national States to a world of 3,000 million people, which may shortly be one of 6,000 million. If the law is to be an effective instrument of freedom and welfare, we must devise new institutional forms, which are not simply a transposition of those of national government, but represent a new epoch in political thinking comparable in historical importance to the creation of the city State, the development of representative institutions and the evolution of federalism.

If and when we achieve such an equilibrium, our satisfaction will be tempered by the knowledge that it cannot last. But the yearning of the human spirit for freedom and welfare is eternal. The extent to which the common law of mankind reflects that yearning at any given time will determine the extent to which it commands general assent, as giving effective expression to the brotherhood of man.

The State and International Organisation
by Professor Roberto Ago (Italy)

Roberto Ago: b.1907. Member, International Law Commission; 1956: Professor of International Law, University of Rome; 1938-1956: University of Milan; 1935-1938: University of Genoa; 1934-1935: University of Catania; 1954-55: Chairman, Governing Body, International Labour Organisation; 1952: Member, Commission of Five Jurists appointed by Council of Europe to draft a European Constitution; member various international conciliation and arbitration commissions; former President, World Federation of United Nations Associations.

In this lecture I propose to share with you some general reflections on an important aspect of the march of international events in our time and, in particular, on certain changes which have occurred in the structure of the international world within a period of less than 50 years.

Let us imagine we are opening a treatise on international law published at the beginning of this century or just before the First World War. If we turn to the chapter on the subjects of international law, we may be sure to find it laid down as a principle that those subjects are sovereign States and only sovereign States. There may be a reference to certain other entities whose right to be regarded as subjects of international law was then under discussion, and mention is sure to be made of the Holy See and the problem of its international status. Unions between States may also be briefly mentioned with a distinction made between various types such as real unions, personal unions, confederacies and federations. In this connexion, the problem of self-governing legal entities may be alluded to, but the discussion will not be carried beyond that point.

Now let us open an up-to-date treatise, reflecting the changes that have taken place in international society. This will confirm that sovereign States are the principal subjects of international law and it will no doubt tell us that there are now nearly three times as many such States as there were in 1914. But the author will certainly draw our attention to another fact, namely that besides States, the Holy See and the recognized unions of States, a completely new category — the international organizations — have made their appearance.

These organizations are, in fact, subjects of international law in their own right and are completely distinct from the sovereign States which are members of them. Their legal powers may be different from those belonging to sovereign States, but their autonomous personality cannot be questioned. It is also an interesting fact that, within a few years, their number has come to exceed that of the sovereign States, which have themselves multiplied so markedly since 1914.

These international organizations are very varied in nature. Some, like the United Nations and the Specialized Agencies, are world-wide. Others are continental, like the Organisation of American States, regional or ethnic, like the Arab League. Their activities may be economic or political or concerned with defence and security. They may deal with finance, agriculture, industry, education, science, health, transportation, telecommunications, aviation or sources of energy.

Such international organizations are formed by States associating for a common purpose. They are legal entities participating in their own right in international life, concluding international agreements and able to appoint representatives with the recognized international privileges and immunities. As individuals associate for a specific object within a State, so States themselves pool some of their resources in a common effort to attain goals which neither the individual nor the single State could achieve.

We have therefore established the fact that the international world of our day is something profoundly different from what it was 50 years ago.

In the first place, we have seen that the number of sovereign States has more than doubled in less than half a century due to the emergence as independent entities of so many nations which were formerly the subjects of other States. This process has affected the structure and legal system of our international society, for all the new countries have their own personalities and special points of view, their own needs, traditions and cultures. While they respect the system of international law brought into existence by the older States, they question some of its premises and they are determined to have their say in its further development or, if necessary, in its revision.

We have also noted the appearance of that new phenomenon, the international organization, as a subject of international law. Does this new arrival on the scene of history constitute merely a passing phase or is it a development of lasting significance? We must attempt a reply to this question, before we examine the effects which the new international organizations are having on international life and law. It will, in fact, be our principal task to inquire into the relations between these two different subjects of international law, sovereign States on the one hand and international organizations on the other.

We must remember that the older international law was the law of a compartmentalized, rather than an organized, society. It corresponded to the characteristics and needs of the kind of international society that existed in practice down to the time of the two world wars. In that society, a limited number of sovereign States, all equal before the law and all extremely jealous of their independence and prerogatives, each rejected any idea of interference from without in their internal affairs. These States maintained constant, and even close, relations with one another and those relations were governed by traditional international law, but they were purely external relations between independent sovereign powers. All States were very chary of admitting the idea that international law, in any form, could penetrate within their frontiers. They were not prepared to let other States tell them what they should do in some particular branch of their internal administration, or to give them instructions regarding their economic, commercial, industrial, agricultural, health, educational or other policies. As far as all of these were concerned, each State was to some extent a *hortus conclusus*.

The rules and regulations laid down by international law were therefore few in number, being limited to the indispensable minimum required for international society to continue to function as a society. Their main purpose was, in fact, to safeguard by reciprocal agreement the independence and freedom of action of States, and simply to try and ensure that the exercise of this freedom by each did not interfere with that of others. It was thus the aim of international law, on the one hand, to seek to avoid friction between sovereign States, and, on the other, to prevent each State from having more than a minimum of influence on the way others ran their national affairs.

It followed from such a concept of the international world that international organizations were regarded as a means of reducing inter-State tensions and of preventing, if possible, the recourse to war. This was still the dominant thought of leaders in the First World War, when planning centered on a possible return to the idea of a Concert of Europe, involving regular meetings of the principal Powers to discuss disputes as they arose and to solve them by the method of compromise. Lord Grey said he regretted there had been no Concert of Europe in 1914, as it might have saved the peace and he looked forward to the establishment of an enlarged and organized Concert after the War.

It was this kind of thinking which lay behind the League Covenant. But, in 1919, we find also a first modest reaching out towards the broader idea which has taken shape in our time — that of a permanent international organization through which States could co-operate all the time and take common action in fields hitherto reserved entirely to their own governments. Such an idea obviously involved some sacrifice of the jealously guarded national sovereignty. For the first time, the essentially negative concept of the co-existence of sovereign States whose principal desire was to be free to act in their own interests as they saw fit, had a rival. Men began to speak in terms of a common action to achieve ends which needed the co-operation of different States working together.

It is true that, even then, this idea was not an entirely new one. As early as 1875 the Universal Postal Union had been founded, in 1878 came a private international organization concerned with meteorology, in 1905 an international organization for agriculture, and in 1907 an international institute of public health. The fact remains, however, that the first really large-scale international organization was the International Labour Office, which came into existence as a result of the Treaty of Versailles. Other important steps taken at about the same time were the creation of the Institute of Intellectual Co-operation, the Health Organisation of the League of Nations, the International Union of Telecommunications, and the Institute for the Unification of Private Law. A little later came the Nansen Office, the Office of the High Commissioner for Refugees and other organs created to meet particular needs. These, however, were still organizations on a small scale.

It was not, in fact, until after the Second World War that this phenomenon of the international organizations took on the proportions we know. After 1945, the principle became generally accepted that sovereign States must not only provide for their mutual co-existence in peace, but also for a growing co-operation between them to reach certain common goals which they could not achieve alone. The post-war problems of economic, social and cultural life brought an understanding that they were, of their very nature, inter-dependent. This, in turn, led to a recognition of the fact that each State needs the co-operation of others and that it cannot alone face up to the tasks confronting it. We now understand why the international organizations have grown so rapidly, and we also feel justified in seeing in that growth evidence that it represents something more significant than a passing phase.

The international organizations would never have come into existence had there not been a widespread realization that certain problems exist in the same, or practically the same, forms over much vaster areas than are enclosed within the frontiers of any single State. It was also realized that serious drawbacks may result from unilateral measures taken independently to deal with such problems. The need for a machinery of co-operation reaching into every continent was born, not from theoretical considerations, but from practical experience. Man saw for himself that some goal desired in Europe could not be fully achieved unless co-ordinated action for the same purpose was taken in the Antipodes. It had become clear that many highly complex problems in finance, trade, social questions, health, communications, transportation and defence cannot be handled effectively in isolation. Economic studies, in particular, played an important part in showing that the riches of the planet, far from being immutably fixed, were a source of wealth which could be increased by joint action. It began also to be understood that economic and social progress in the economically less favoured regions of the world is a necessssary condition for the continuation of such progress in countries which have already reached an advanced stage. Humanitarian feelings alone need not be the only motive impelling the economically developed countries to extend a helping hand to others.

All these considerations enable us to see why the United Nations family of organizations was not conceived like the League of Nations, mainly as an organ for the settlement of international disputes, but rather as one for promoting co-operation in all fields where valuable results could be expected. The same considerations explain the successful launching of organizations such as the Regional Economic Commissions, the Technical Assistance Board, the Special Fund, the Office of the High Commissioner for Refugees, the Relief and Works Agency for Refugees in Palestine, that for the rehabilitation of Korea and dozens of others.

They apply as powerfully to the creation and influence of all the specialized agencies such as the International Labour Organisation, the Food and Agriculture Organization of the United Nations, the United Nations Educational, Scientific and Cultural Organization, the International Bank for Reconstruction and Development, the International Monetary Fund, the International

Civil Aviation Organization, the World Health Organization, the International Telecommunication Union, the World Meteorological Organization, the Interim Commission for International Trade Organization/General Agreement on Tariffs and Trade, and the International Atomic Energy Agency. This list does not, of course, include the imposing number of regional organizations, both European and non-European, some with a numerous, and some with a smaller membership, or all the long line of technical institutions not included in the UN family.

Membership in these various international organizations inevitably tends to restrict the freedom of States, for the organizations are continually taking action in fields where only a short time ago each State exercised unchallenged authority. In fact, nowadays, side by side with each of the governmental Ministries or each branch of a national administration there exists an international organization, or even a number of such organizations, active in the same field.

How far and in what way does the action of these international organizations harmonize with that of individual member States? To what extent is the free action of States limited in our time by the intervention of international organizations?

The activity of these organizations usually takes one of two forms. The first method by which an international organization penetrates into the domestic life of a sovereign State is through the channel of the law. It does so by legally binding all its members to take within their own borders steps agreed upon by the majority as desirable to attain a certain objective. Among the essential functions of the United Nations and the specialized agencies is to secure the adoption of a series of international conventions coming within their respective areas of competence. If these permanent organizations did not exist, the preparation and international adoption of such conventions would be extremely difficult and time-absorbing. When, however, an international organization can undertake the preliminary preparation of a draft convention, can have it considered at the periodical meetings of legally constituted assemblies, and can then use its influence to secure ratification of such a convention, the result is a very great increase in the number of such international agreements that can be adopted. And the fields covered by them are continually being extended. A further advantage is that an international organization can ensure uniformity in the legislation and policies of many different States — the 104 International Labour Conventions adopted since the First World War are an excellent illustration of this. The older international law is thus being supplemented by an ever more complex network of legally binding obligations which States are assuming in fields where they have abandoned, no doubt for ever, their former complete freedom of action.

Yet this is only one way by which the international organizations are penetrating into the national life of sovereign States. The second method consists of what has come to be called the "operational" activities of the organizations. Experience showed that it was not enough for States to agree to bring their practice in certain fields into line with that of others. Countries might be full of goodwill, but might lack the physical resources, and capital and skilled personnel to carry out desirable measures or to implement programmes on which all were agreed. It was therefore found necessary to call upon many of the international organizations for help in certain practical activities, most of which are covered by the term "technical assistance". The purpose of this intervention by the organizations has been to help many States to carry out tasks which they could never hope to realize alone. This help is, of course, given mainly to the economically less developed countries of the world and it is enabling them to profit with a minimum of delay from the rich experience and knowledge of others.

In certain cases, the international organizations are, now, not simply helping governments by advice to achieve certain results, but even taking over some of their responsibilities for a while because, alone, those governments could not assume the burden. The United Nations Korean Reconstruction Agency undertook such special responsibilities to help in the rehabilitation of the Republic of Korea, and with these we might compare the activities of UNRRA and the International Refugee Organization.

Such organizations were actually created to deal with practical problems, of an emergency nature, which were too big for the resources of States immediately concerned. We are now reaching the stage where such abnormal situations are no longer required to justify direct, operational activities by the international organizations, which are coming to regard these activities as routine operations. More and more of the time and money of the organizations is, in fact, being devoted to these ends.

The international organizations are thus becoming operative in areas once strictly reserved to national governments, and they are doing this more and more obviously and in various ways. The historical significance of these developments will escape no one. In half a century the independent, sovereign State which, in the preceding centuries, had done so much to absorb political entities within its borders, has in turn been obliged to admit the existence of broader organizations than its own, to follow their instructions, to seek their assistance and sometimes even to stand aside and allow them, because of its own admitted incapacity, to act in its place. It goes without saying that some States are so powerful and well-endowed that they have much less need of the international organizations and their help, but none can do without their co-operation. In our world no State can dispense entirely with the co-operation of others. The traditional notion of independence, as expressed in the word "sovereignty", is gradually giving way to a fresh concept. States in our world remain sovereign States. They still keep their independence and their equality in law. They are less than ever disposed to tolerate a situation in which one country depends on another. At the same time, they are more and more willing to recognize the inter-dependence of the whole community of nations. They have come to understand that nations can no longer be self-contained, and that the international organizations are there to offer them the co-operation without which the march of progress would be arrested for them.

Because of the rapidity with which the international organizations have evolved, there have been inevitable errors. There have been waste, overlapping, uncertain policies. Nevertheless, one fact remains paramount. Man has understood in our lifetime that the phenomenon of international organization is perhaps the most important legal and social characteristic of our age. Despite all obstacles, all divisions and all clashes of interest, the movement of the world towards unity is progressively gathering speed. We must not assume that the society of the future will come into being at the leisurely pace which marked historic growth in earlier centuries. In our age of cosmic rockets, history seems to be taking fright. For fear of being left behind, it has changed from a canter to a frenzied gallop.

Liberty and Law in International Life
by Dag Hammarskjold

A lecture delivered at the annual convention of the American Bar Association in Philadelphia, 22 August 1955.
Dag Hammarskjold: b.1905, d.1961. 1953-1961: Secretary-General of the United Nations; 1951-1953: member of Swedish delegations to Sixth and Seventh Sessions of United Nations General Assembly; 1951: Minister without Portfolio; 1949: Secretary-General of Foreign Office; 1948: chief delegate to conference of Organization for European Economic Co-operation, Paris; 1941-1948: Chairman, Board of Swedish National Bank, and Permanent Under-Secretary, Ministry of Finance; 1954: elected member of Swedish Academy.

I. Introduction

It is a pleasure for me to speak today to an eminent group of lawyers on a legal subject, and I feel indebted to Judge Edmonds for having given me an opportunity to do so. I grew up in a family much concerned with law, especially international law, and I myself studied law in my country. I therefore do not feel that I am coming here as a stranger, unacquainted with the problems and aspirations which are yours.

Law is the most advanced of the bodies of techniques which men have worked out for a living together in an orderly and harmonious way. It is well developed as a system for balancing the interests of the individual with the interests of society. I am convinced that the techniques of law can be adapted and applied more fully than at present also to the society of States. Lawyers have the special knowledge, skills and experience which enable them to contribute much both to the study of the problems involved in this development and to promoting public acceptance of new steps forward. I shall speak later of the kind of work which I think they could well undertake to this end. I should like first, however, to say something about the problem, as I see it, of developing a stronger and more satisfactory international law in the present society of States, so that a system of ordered liberty under law may be established in international relations.

II. The Society of States
A. The nature of individual States

A State is a living, functioning organism. It forms a sociological, psychological and economic unit of which men passionately feel themselves to be parts. A State's citizens have the habit of living and working together. They have a sense of community based on a body of shared values, traditions and aspirations. In our world of today, due to the influence of many factors, a new international consciousness is beginning to develop. Men increasingly realize that they have an allegiance to mankind as a whole as well as to their own sections of it. But it will take a considerable time before this feeling gains such strength as to influence fundamentally the present nature of international relations.

Thus, if we are realists, we will have to make the best of a world emotionally as well as legally divided into national States. Most men will no doubt continue to wish to deal with as many of the important concerns of life as possible within their own nations, where there is a greater degree of community of values and feelings than in the world at large. If plans for international order are to have any chance of acceptance they must leave as great an area of liberty to States as possible.

B. Sovereignty (liberty) and the international society

Of course, there is not now and never has been any such thing as unlimited liberty, or sovereignty, either for an individual or for a State. Each man's freedom is limited by that of his neighbours. No State has ever had complete freedom to accomplish whatever it desires, without the possibility of frustration by another will. The very existence of a society, or — in the international field — of a community of nations, imposes certain limitations on the freedom of action of all its members, no matter how loose or disorderly the society or communities may be. Limitations on the sovereignty of nations, as on the liberty of individuals, are thus inevitable. There is, however, a considerable choice as to their extent and kind.

The society may tend on the one hand toward a brutal anarchy where might is always right, and where clumsy force perpetually runs the risk of starting an armed conflict which would destroy not only the possibility of gaining the aims sought by the contestants, but probably the contestants themselves. Or, on the other hand, the society may tend, within the limits of human imperfections, to liberty under law, where inevitable conflicts of interest are resolved by orderly and rational deliberation so as to reconcile the conflicting interests with each other and with the interests of the society as a whole. Either of these extremes is difficult to reach; moral feelings, principles, and habits of procedure will always play a part in international relations, and so will the realities of power. But everyone who can have any influence on the policy of a government has a choice as to which tendency he wishes to favour.

For States as well as for individuals the only kind of liberty worth having is liberty under law. The familiar paradox that freedom can be preserved only by setting limits to it is as true of the society of States as of societies of men. Many analogies between the two kinds of society tend to be misleading, because the larger the human group that is acting, the more complicated are the principles of politics, economics and even psychology which govern the action. But in this case the analogy is sound; order is necessary for enjoyment of the fruits of liberty, and order requires surrender of the freedom to impair the freedom of others. The truest safeguard of sovereignty in an interdependent world is therefore an effective international law.

The strengthening of international law is consequently in the long-term interest of States, even though it might occasionally conflict with short-term interests. Since the life of States is measured in centuries and their activities are manifold, statesmen have every reason to take a long-range objective view. Though disorder may profit their States today in one case it may hurt them in another tomorrow, and in the long run is bound to work them harm.

III. The present state of international law

However, when we look at the present role of international law in world affairs it is difficult to feel that there has been the degree of progress there should have been in the past twenty-five years, and in some fields it could be said that there has been a regression. Nearly as many cases have been submitted to judicial settlement and arbitration as in the past, but the fact remains that the International Court of Justice is still not adequately used by States. Only about half the Members of the United Nations have accepted the compulsory jurisdiction of the Court, despite a resolution of the General Assembly urging them to do so. Even where compulsory jurisdiction exists, it is rarely invoked. The present Court has been asked for only eight advisory opinions in ten years, while its predecessor was asked for twenty-six in the same length of time.

The other organs of the United Nations, faced with the manifold problems of a new system of international cooperation in a troubled period, have found it necessary to keep as flexible as possible. The result has been that though the beginnings have been made of a "common law" of the United Nations based on the application of the Charter, this growth has not been as extensive nor as solid as might have been hoped and expected at the Organisation's birth.

Furthermore, at a deeper level, there has been a good deal of upsetting of the rules themselves in many of the traditional fields of international law. For example, who today could assume, as was done by some writers at the beginning of the twentieth century, that there is any consensus on the three-mile limit of territorial waters, or on many aspects of the treatment of foreigners and foreign investments? This unsettling of the old law has accompanied great changes in the structure of international relations, and is mainly a necessary phase of the growth of the law and of its adaptation to new circumstances.

But the same period that has seen some destruction of old law has also seen the most important, the most revolutionary development in the law which has occurred since the seventeenth century, and that is the outlawry of aggressive force as a means of settling disputes. Though many of the details and consequences of this new rule remain to be worked out, the rule itself is firmly established and it may serve as an indication of how law may grow under the impulsion of the moral feelings of mankind.

We should also bear in mind that international law is generally observed. In all the complexity and multiplicity of modern international relations, where thousands of actions on the international plane are taken every day, it is rare that a violation of the law is even alleged to have occurred. By and large States, like individuals, quietly obey the law in their activities because obedience to law is a habit, from which for many reasons it is unwise to depart.

IV. Reasons why legal techniques are not more used

Nevertheless, as I have said, the law and legal techniques are not now used as much as they should be by States in their relations with one another. Again and again the law is denied a function in international disputes either on the ground that they are "political" or "non-justiciable," or by a tacit assumption that legal methods are not appropriate. What substance is there in the claim that legal solutions are not appropriate in large categories of disputes?

In adversary proceedings before a court, it is, in a purely technical sense, possible to decide nearly any dispute on the basis of law. If one State claims that another has an obligation to act in a certain way, a decision can almost always be made as to whether the claim is or is not legally justified, no matter how incomplete the legal system may be from some points of view.

There is thus no technical legal reason why most international disputes should not be submitted to judicial settlement, but there are other reasons, both good and bad. One good reason may be that the dispute relates to the area of liberty of States, in which the law leaves them free to choose their course of action. This area, of course, includes matters which are clearly international; examples which may be drawn from issues before the United Nations relate to some of the aspects of international economic development, and to some of the differences in the highly controversial field of self-determination. In matters like these the important issues are political, economic and even moral; they could not very well be settled by a court, which is expert only in the law.

There are disputes, however, in which the existing law really covers all or some of the issues, but where those concerned simply do not wish to settle on the basis of law, though they admit its binding force. This attitude is not necessarily misguided. It may be desired to settle by conciliation, and it may be thought that a clear definition of the rights of the parties would leave too little flexibility for negotiation to bring them together. But a clarification of the legal position can often help when the positions of the parties are too far apart to be reconciled. Moreover, a negotiated solution that ignores the legal issues is just as unlikely to be permanent as a solution that ignores any other main aspect of the case; a party which is induced to accept a settlement without any consideration of its legal claims is likely to retain an abiding sense of injustice.

Again, the parties themselves may wish to preserve or improve their positions rather than to settle at the risk of losing their claims. This attitude is prevalent in times of great tension such as those we have been living through, when short-range interests tend to seem all-important. It is also prevalent in times of intense nationalism, when States which have recently entered the international society are sensitive to anything that appears to affect their newly acquired independence and even in older States public feeling on international issues is deeply aroused. Old arbitration treaties from before the First World War exclude matters of "vital national interest" or matters "affecting the national honour" from the obligation to arbitrate. The state of mind that led to writing these provisions still persists.

Moreover, in occasional cases the law may cease to be in accordance with widely accepted notions of justice. The law is a stable element in society, and as such it often tends to preserve the *status quo*. An old legal situation may come, however, to be out of harmony with new aspirations or moral feelings. When this happens in a national society, new legislation normally offers opportunities to create a more generally satisfactory state of the law. To arrive at an agreement on a change of a rule of international law or on the introduction of a new rule, however, has not been so easy. Therefore, the kind of development that inside a State would find expression in a legislative reform sometimes tends on the international level to take the form of a departure in action from what is still considered to be the law.

V. Ways in which the law should be more developed and used

This year has brought new hope of a relaxation of some of the most important tensions which have divided the world. International relations may be entering a new and more stable stage. If this new stage comes to pass, the time will be propitious for a development of international order on the basis of a wider use of law. As international cooperation increases, so necessarily will the development of the law, by which international cooperation is organized and given a stable framework. The development of the law is not an end to be sought for itself, but is a means by which other ends may be attained in an orderly and lasting way. When the international society becomes able to agree on the ends to be sought in dealing with some of the complex problems which face it, practical solutions can be worked out, with all necessary adjustments and compromises. These solutions can thus be given a legal form so as to govern the conduct of States. I expect that the United Nations as the only permanent instrument for co-operation on a world-wide scale in dealing with major political problems will play a large part in these developments.

One of the most important political problems on which progress is needed is the working out of the specific applications and consequences of the new rule of law which outlaws aggressive force.

Without such a development the law against aggression may remain an illusory generality. Moreover, it will be difficult to uphold unless States are really willing to settle their disputes by peaceful means, instead of leaving them to fester and poison international relations. It is provided in Article 33 of the Charter, at the opening of the chapter on the pacific settlement of disputes by the Security Council, that

> "The parties to any dispute, the continuance of which is likely to endanger the maintenance of international peace and security, shall first of all, seek a solution by negotiation, enquiry, mediation, conciliation, arbitration, judicial settlement, resort to regional agencies or arrangements, or other peaceful means of their own choice."

The Members of the United Nations must give a new and serious consideration to this obligation and to the means of fulfilling it. What better, what more encouraging expression could be given to the new spirit of which we seem to see a dawn.

There are other ways in which the law should be more widely used in the United Nations. In the first place, I hope that more disputes will be referred to the International Court of Justice. This is an effective means both of settling disputes and of developing the law. The Court and its predecessor have over the past thirty-odd years established and developed a high judicial tradition. The Court's record is one of the best made by any international organ. One cannot look into the collection of the judgements and advisory opinions of the Court and its predecessor without being impressed by a work outstanding for intellectual power, breadth of view, scrupulous impartiality, adherence to the best traditions of the law, and enlightened statesmanship.

There may, however, be issues of a highly technical nature which States may prefer to bring before *ad hoc* arbitral tribunals. Such tribunals also make possible procedures allowing, for example, individuals to bring limited classes of claims directly against States.

The political or other non-legal elements of an issue or dispute may make it preferable to bring it before an organ of the United Nations other than the Court. I hope that the law will play a larger part in the discussions of these organs. There are several ways in which it should do so. In the first place, the beginnings which have been made of a law based on practice concerning the interpretation and application of the United Nations Charter should be strengthened and developed. The Charter, like any other constitutional instrument, slowly grows and changes with application, and further attention to this growth is needed. The elements of stability and predictability, of establishing and following sound precedents, can well be increased in the proceedings of the United Nations as the world political situation grows more stable. This will promote orderly consideration of issues, and will make the Organization more able to profit by its past experience.

In the second place, the United Nations should devote more attention to the application of international law to issues before it. Apart from the Court, the organs of the United Nations do not have a judicial character and their methods must be primarily political. But a clarification of the legal issues, which are an important part of any dispute where they are present, can often facilitate a solution. This can be done either by requesting an advisory opinion from the International Court of Justice, by referring the matter to the Legal Committee of the General Assembly, or, if a less formal method seems appropriate, by the appointment of a committee of jurists.

In the third place, the United Nations is, as I have said, the most appropriate place for development and change of international law on behalf of the whole society of States. One method of doing so might be the conclusion of multilateral conventions. In fields where the time is not yet ripe for a convention, however, a less binding method may be used, such as a declaration of existing law with the force of a recommendation, or a declaration setting a standard as a commonly agreed goal for aspiration. Moreover, the General Assembly has special functions under the Charter concerning the codification and progressive development of international law, and has established the International Law Commission to promote these aims. The Commission's work is of high importance, and should in all its phases be given the most careful and sympathetic consideration by States. To leave the work of the Commission open to undue political influences or to discourage it by neglect would be to operate against some of the most vital interests of the community of nations.

VI. What lawyers can do

The greater use and development of international law are matters which depend in the first instance on States. They are the masters in the field, and can arrange their relations so as to maintain ordered freedom, or so as to bring about anarchy. The machinery of international cooperation — the United Nations and other international institutions — is theirs to use for its proper purposes, to distort for the opposite purposes or to leave idle.

The policy of States is, however, the ultimate responsibility of citizens. It is therefore desirable that the legal profession in the various countries should bring to public attention the legal issues arising for their own and other countries, and should examine the desirability and appropriate methods of settlement on the basis of law. The legal profession is the part of the national community where it is most appropriate that a public consciousness of the importance of international law and of the desirability of its greater use should develop. It has been said that the average man has much less knowledge of the way international law affects his life and his country than of how national law affects them. The Bar can do much to improve this situation. Moreover, a country's lawyers, skilled as they are in the organization of their own society, are particularly qualified to understand the national background of international relations, and to see how their country, while retaining its proper freedom to solve its own problems in its own way, can cooperate with other countries in the furtherance of international order.

Furthermore, ideas and proposals worked out by technically qualified unofficial groups often come to have a great influence on the policy of governments. There can never be too much informed discussion on the basic principles of international relations, including the part which is actually played and should come to be played by the law. Also, a discussion of particular rules will help to show what they are at present, and whether they should be developed or altered.

All of these problems are very suitable for study and discussion by members of the Bar. Such study and discussion are the principal ways in which lawyers may contribute to the development of an international order which will effectively protect both the freedom of individual States and the peace of the international society as a whole.

Dag Hammarskjold and the Relation of Law to Politics
by Oscar Schachter

Oscar Schachter: b. 1915. Director, General Legal Division, UN Office of Legal Affairs; former Attorney, U. S. Department of Labor, Washington; Principal Divisional Assistant, U. S. Department of State serving as adviser on war-time economic controls and on European liberated areas; Assistant General Counsel, UNRRA.

The sudden and tragic death of Dag Hammarskjold on September 17, 1961, evoked throughout almost the entire world a sense of grief and loss that was without parallel in recent times. In the tributes paid him there was universal recognition of his extraordinary personal qualities: the depth and brilliance of his intellect, his strength of spirit, dedication, courage, and incredible stamina. He was that rare, indeed almost incomparable, combination of a man who could act with energy, boldness and consummate skill in meeting the harsh conflicts of our time, and at the same time could lead a life of inner contemplation and aesthetic experience. For those privileged to work closely with him, he had a contagious vitality and zest which, even in the most discouraging moments, inspired renewed effort. He brought to these personal qualities a tough-minded awareness of political realities and a talent for creative political innovation. The result was an era of international action in which the United Nations moved from the plane of words to that of deeds in facing some of the most perilous crises of this generation. It may well be that, with the death of Mr. Hammarskjold, this era has come to a close, but it is not likely that its example will be forgotten.

While Dag Hammarskjold's accomplishments have been justifiably regarded as essentially political and diplomatic, their implications for the development of international law merit special consideration. He regarded himself as a man of law, in part because of his formal legal training, in part, it seemed, because of his intellectual delight in the subtleties of legal analysis. There was also perhaps an element of personal sentiment in his attitude, for he had a manifest pride in his family's legal background and especially in the contribution made by his father, Hjalmar Hammarskjold,[1] and his brother, Ake.[2] Much more important, however, than these considerations was the conviction, which he increasingly expressed, that the processes of law, and, as he put it, the principles of justice were crucial to the effort to avert disaster and to achieve a secure and decent international order. That this conviction went far deeper than the conventional homage paid to the rule of law soon became evident to one who shared his professional interest. It was more than a belief in a distant age paid to the rule of law soon became evident to the one who shared his professional interest. It was more than a belief in a distant goal; it inspired and influenced his actions from day to day, and it is not surprising that one of the first tributes paid him by an ambassador who knew him well was to describe him as "imbued with the spirit of law".

It may be asked whether the "spirit of law" or a belief in the value of the legal process can have much practical significance in an intensely political atmosphere such as that of the United Nations. There are, of course, many who answer in the negative; they see no meaningful application of law except in terms of an effective judicial system, and they regard references to "law" in a political body as no more than rhetorical flourishes without influence on actual conduct or policy. Hammarskjold's beliefs and his practical actions were in a sense a challenge to this view for they affirmed the importance of law in the United Nations while acknowledging the realities of power and political pres-

[1] Hjalmar J. L. Hammarskjold, who was the Prime Minister of Sweden during the first World War, served as the Chairman of the Committee of Experts for the Progressive Codification of International Law of the League of Nations, and as President of the International Law Association.

[2] Ake Hammarskjold was the Registrar of the Permanent Court of International Justice from 1922 to 1936, and a Judge of that Court in 1936-1937.

sures. To demonstrate this more specifically, an attempt will be made to summarize, under four headings, what seem to be the fundamental conceptions of Hammarskjold's approach to the relation of law and politics in contemporary international society. These conceptions, it will be seen, differ substantially from the traditional views of international lawyers and place in fresh perspective some of the pervasive dilemmas of international politics.

1. Law as a Source and Basis of Policy

Hammarskjold made no sharp distinction between law and policy; in this he departed clearly from the prevailing positivist approach. He viewed the body of law not merely as a technical set of rules and procedures, but as the authoritative expression of principles that determine the goals and direction of collective action. This did not mean, of course, that he considered that legal precepts alone expressed the aims of states, or that they automatically determined the decisions of international bodies irrespective of other considerations. He recognized that, in international society as in domestic, legal norms are one class of many factors that enter into the process of decision-making. But, while acknowledging the influence of other factors, he laid stress on the binding character of the legal element, and consequently on the priority that should be accorded to it over other interests and claims. This was not merely a theoretical point of view: his record is replete with instances in which he found that the principles of the Charter, general and comprehensive as they are, provided sufficient guidance to enable him to resolve concrete controversies.[3] Faced with conflicting national demands and ex-

---

[3]Some examples were mentioned by Mr. Hammarskjold in a footnote to his lecture, "The International Civil Servant in Law and in Fact," given at Oxford University on 30 May, 1961 (Clarendon Press). The footnote refers to the fact that the principles and purposes of the Charter are specific enough to have practical significance in concrete cases. It reads:
"1. See, for example, references to the Charter in relation to the establishment and operation of UNEF: U.N. Doc. A/3302, General Assembly, Official Records, First Emergency Special Session, Annexes, Agenda Item 5, pp. 19-23; U.N. Doc. A/3512, General Assembly, Official Records, Eleventh Session, Annexes, Agenda Item 66, pp. 47-50. See also references to the Charter in relation to the question of the Congo: U.N. Doc. S/PV. 887, p. 17; U.N. Doc. S/PV. 920, p. 47; U.N. Doc. S/PV. 942, pp. 137-40; U.N. Doc S/4637 A."

pectations, he relied on these principles and on other generally accepted legal concepts as a manifestation of the long-range major policies to which all governments had committed themselves. He did this not merely in deference to formal authority, but on the premise that the fundamental principles of the Charter and international law embodied the deeply-held values of the great majority of mankind and therefore constituted the moral, as well as the legal, imperatives of international life. In the main, he saw them "as a projection into the international arena and international community of purposes and principles already accepted as being of national validity."[4]

2. Principles and Flexibility

Hammarskjold's reliance on principles and legal concepts may appear to be at variance with the flexibility and adroitness that characterized much of his political activity; yet on reflection it will be seen that these apparently antithetical approaches were both essential aspects of a skilled technique for dealing with the specific problems which he faced. It is a technique that should be of special interest to the international lawyer, for it demonstrated that legal norms can be applied to novel situations without rigidity or blind conformity to precedent.

That Hammarskjold was able to do this may be attributed to three factors. One was that his own cast of mind and philosophic approach were congenial to the interplay between principles and contingent fact; he invariably sought for norms but he was equally mindful of the variety, flux and novelty of actual events. A second factor was his conception of his office. A fundamental tenet was that the exclusively international responsibility of the Secretary General implied above all a firm adherence to the principles of the Charter and other standards accepted as binding by Member States. Only through principled behavior could he fulfill his obligation of impartiality and avoid the risks of partisan and special pleading.

[4]"Introduction to the Sixteenth Annual Report of the Secretary-General on the Work of the Organization, 1960-1961," in 8 *United Nations Review* 12-17, 34-35 (September 1961), published by the U.N. Office of Public Information, OPI/79.

At the same time he realized that he was not a judge, called upon to pass judgement on the propriety of state conduct. He regarded himself essentially as a diplomat, a political technician who was required from time to time to deal with specific problems. The fact that these problems arose frequently in situations of crisis was the third factor influential in Hammarskjold's approach. For the element of "crisis" meant that there was strong pressure to meet the necessities of the particular problem and to avoid the adoption of formulae that might have unforeseen implications in future cases. It was this third factor that called for the *ad hoc* solution and the supple application of general rules.

The technique of fusing these opposing elements into workable solutions cannot be easily described; it is more art than engineering and blueprints are not likely to be available. Certainly, an essential feature lay in the nature of the general rules which guided him. They were, in the main, principles derived from Articles 1 and 2 of the Charter; on that basis, they already commanded, in a psychological and political sense, high priority among the values formally accepted by the governments of the world. They were flexible in that they did not impose specific procedural patterns or detailed machinery for action; they left room for adaptation to the particular needs and the resources available for a given undertaking.

A good example is seen in the guiding principles which Hammarskjold derived from the experience of the United Nations Emergency Force in Gaza, and which he summarized in a report to the General Assembly.[5] He cautioned against a mechanical repetition of the UNEF formula, and indicated the factors which might require a different pattern in the future. However, he also considered that, by distilling the UNEF experience, it was possible to arrive at fundamental criteria which would provide standards and guidelines for future undertakings and consequently facilitate their adoption by the United Nations organs. It was not long before this was tested in the Security Council proceedings dealing with the request for military assistance in the Congo.

[5]General Assembly, Official Records, Thirteenth Session, Annexes, Agenda Item 65, U.N. Doc. A/3943.

The precise UNEF arrangement did not fit the Congo, but the guiding principles derived from that experience were advanced by the Secretary General and accepted by the governments as the constitutional basis of the United Nations operation in the Congo. The principles included that of non-intervention in internal political conflicts, the exclusion of the major military Powers from the Force, the international character and status of the Force, the independence of the United Nations in the selection of such troops, and the concept of good faith in the interpretation of the purposes of the Force.[6] The fact that these principles had been formulated in advance enabled the Secretary General at the outset to clarify the legal and practical basis of the Force for the Congo and provided a strengthened foundation for action by the governments. General as these principles might appear to be when stated in the abstract, the experience in the Congo demonstrated that they could have effect in projecting specific policies to be followed and in restraining ill-considered measures.

It is also of significance in evaluating Hammarskjold's flexibility that he characteristically expressed basic principles in terms of opposing tendencies (applying, one might say, the philosophic concept of polarity or dialectical opposition). He never lost sight of the fact that a principle, such as that of observance of human rights, was balanced by the concept of non-intervention, or that the notion of equality of states had to be considered in a context which included the special responsibilities of the great Powers. The fact that such precepts had contradictory implications meant that they could not provide automatic answers to particular problems, but rather that they served as criteria which had to be weighed and balanced in order to achieve a rational solution of the particular problem. Paul Freund gave eloquent expression to this idea in regard to the abstractions in American constitutional law:

> "These abstractions, arrayed in intransigent hostility like robot sentinels facing each other across a border, can become use-

---

[6]See U.N. Doc. S/PV. 873, pp. 11-12. For a more detailed discussion of these principles, see Miller, "Legal Aspects of the United Nations Action in the Congo," 55 A.J.I.L. 1 (1961).

ful guardians on either hand in the climb to truth if they can be made to march together. Somehow the life blood of the concrete problem tempers the mechanical arrogance of abstractions."[7]

While this theme was not explicitly formulated by Hammarskjold, it runs through his statements and his actions. He recognized that there was inevitably a tension between principles and concrete needs; his actions showed that, by taking account of both, he sought to achieve "that combination of steadfastness of purpose and flexibility of approach which alone can guarantee that the possibilities which we are exploring will have been tested to the full."[8]

3. The Relation between Law and Diplomacy

Hammarskjold conceived of his office primarily in terms of diplomacy, a "quiet" diplomacy which he conducted, as Walter Lippmann observed, with "a finesse and courtliness in the great traditions of Europe." But the setting and purposes of that diplomacy were far from the traditional. In Lippmann's eloquent appraisal: "Never before and perhaps never again has any man used the intense art of diplomacy for such unconventional and novel experiments."[9] Whether unconventional or traditional, diplomacy is normally regarded as separate from — indeed, some would say opposed to — the processes of law, and many have warned against mingling the two. Yet the experience of Hammarskjold indicates that this is an oversimplified view, and that a properly balanced combination of law and diplomacy may be an advantage, even at times a necessity.

The advantage of a legal basis is perhaps most evident when

---

[7] 69 Harvard Law Review 803 (1956). The same conception of polarity is applied by Professor Myres S. McDougal in his many original contributions to international law. See, for example, McDougal and Feliciano, "Legal Regulation of Resort to International Coercion," 68 *Yale Law Journal* 1057 (1959), and other essays in *Studies in World Public Order* (Yale University Press, 1960).

[8] Address delivered by Mr. Hammarskjold at the University of Chicago Law School, entitled "The Development of a Constitutional Framework for International Co-operation", in 6 *United Nations Review* 26-30 (June 1960), published by U.N. Office of Public Information, OPI/37.

[9] *New York Herald Tribune*, 21 Sept. 1961.

one considers the initial stage of a conciliation or good offices effort. It is apparent that a third party cannot enter the delicate terrain of inter-State controversy without having a *locus standi* acceptable to the parties directly concerned. Sometimes this is simply satisfied by the willingness of the parties to accept a friendly third-part intermediary; far more frequently, there are objections to any conciliation efforts, and influential groups within the States concerned (or perhaps external forces) may make it difficult for the government to agree to a third-party "volunteer." However, when the third party is buttressed by firm legal authority — that is, when his *locus standi* rests on the rules and procedures to which that State has formally committed itself, that in itself becomes a cogent factor in overcoming resistance. Diplomatic intervention may then be viewed as part of generally accepted procedures agreed to by all States, and consequently involving no invidious connotation for the party to the dispute. Hammarskjold had a profound appreciation of this aspect of peaceful settlement, and he therefore attached considerable importance to the grant of authority enabling him to enter into private discussions. He recognized in this respect the legal significance of the Security Council's responsibilities under the Charter, and he laid stress on the importance of a mandate by that organ in sitnations involving threats to the peace.[10] In point of fact, most of his diplomatic activities, notably in the Middle East, Africa and Southeast Asia, were undertaken on the basis of a mandate of the Security Council, bolstered in several cases by agreements of the parties themselves. Only rarely did he offer his good offices without a Security Council or General Assembly mandate, and these instances were limited to situations in which both sides desired his participation in preliminary discussions.[11]

There is another, no less important, aspect of the relation between law and diplomacy which can be discerned in Hammarskjold's diplomatic technique. An examination of his conciliation

[10] See address by Mr. Hammarskjold to the Students' Association of Copenhagen, entitled "Do We Need the United Nations?", in 5 *United Nations Review* 22-26 (June 1959), published by U.N. Office of Public Information.
[11] Introduction to the Fourteenth Annual Report of the Secretary General on the Work of the Organization, 1958-1959, U.N. Doc. A/4132/Add. 1, p. 3.

efforts shows that he relied to a considerable extent on establishing a common ground of principles to which both sides could adhere. An essential element in this process was to suggest general standards which had a legal quality, whether as an accepted norm of international law or as a rule which was implied by or closely related to a principle of law. The legal aspect was important in achieving acceptance because it endowed the proposed standards with the authority of pre-existing obligations and the character of a universal rule that would be applied equally in other cases. It thus implied that the solution to be reached would not diverge too sharply from the probable expectations of the States concerned, and for that reason was less likely to involve political difficulties. It also offered an assurance that the conciliation effort was carried out with objectivity and impartiality and therefore without discrimination against either side. Hammarskjold's awareness of these factors is demonstrated by his frequent recourse to legal rules and precedents which, directly or by analogy, could be applied to the particular situation and accepted as guiding principles by the parties concerned. By a discriminating and skillful use of legal principles, he was thus able to further his diplomacy of conciliation and by its success to reinforce the effectiveness of law.

4. Law, Power and Action

Although Hammarskjold often stressed the imperative quality of legal norms, this did not mean that he regarded law as an autonomous force which develops and is applied independently of political and social factors. He preferred to view law not as a "construction of ideal patterns," but in an "organic sense,"[12] as an institution which grows in response to felt necessities and within the limits set by historical conditions and human attitudes. Placed as he was in the center of the political maelstrom, Hammarskjold could not but be keenly aware of the impact of power relations on the normative structure of international society. He was especially mindful of the fact that the constitutional

[12]See address of Mr. Hammarskjold referred to in note 8 above.

pattern of the United Nations had been molded largely by the concentration of power in the two major blocs and by the deep conflict between them. He was equally aware of the extent to which internal instability and the demands for radical changes affected the application of existing rules of public order. But it was characteristic that he regarded these factors not merely as imposing limits on the use of law, but in a more positive sense as a challenge which called for creative attempts to find new norms and procedures. In making these attempts in new directions, Hammarskjold never lost sight of the limiting conditions; he always was conscious that he was nurturing an organic growth, not designing an ideal pattern.

He did not, therefore, attempt to set law against power. He sought rather to find within the limits of power the elements of common interest on the basis of which joint action and agreed standards could be established. In the area of advancing technologies, such as atomic energy and outer space, he pursued efforts to develop new normative arrangements based on the acknowledged factors of interdependence. In the economic and social field, he stressed the mutual interest of the advanced states in combatting the debasement of living standards and human dignity in the impoverished countries of the world. In the most critical arena, the relation between the major power blocs, he devoted himself to seeking balanced arrangements based on the mutual interest of both blocs to survive in a world in which each possessed the power to destroy the other. He did not endeavor to enter directly into big-Power relations, nor in any way to mediate directly between them. But he found opportunities in the peripheral areas, especially in the "power vacuums" that arose in underdeveloped areas and which provoked external intervention and the inevitable counteraction by the other side.[13] In these matters he sought to stave off the dangerous spiral of action and reaction by measures to fill the vacuums and create a viable economy and government by means of economic and financial aid, the building of governmental and administrative machinery, the

[13] Introduction to the Fifteenth Annual Report of the Secretary-General on the Work of the Organization, 1959-1960, U.N. Doc. A/4390/Add. 1, p. 4.

provision of educational and technical training, and, even as in the Congo, by using armed force to maintain internal order. These measures, commonly described as "executive action," signified for Hammarskjold a fundamental and decisive advance toward a more effective system of international cooperation, and they have been widely regarded as constituting a major feature of his political legacy.

Although these "operational" measures do not at first seem to be related to international law, it will be evident on reflection that they have an impact on the evolution of standards of international behavior, and the effective implementation of such standards. For it must be borne in mind that collective intervention of the kind described, based on United Nations principles, involves more than "action." It necessarily includes new conceptions of permissible and impermissible interference by individual States, and of the Charter obligations for mutual assistance and co-operation. Moreover, such measures constitute, as Mr. Hammarskjold observed, practical means and techniques for bringing about compliance with international decisions and principles. They can, therefore, be regarded in a broader and more subtle sense, as a part of the enforcement or sanctioning machinery which is available to the international community to assure observance of its decisions. Viewed in these terms, such practical action will be seen as imparting a new dimension to the efforts to give vigor and efficacy to a normative structure based on the common interests of all peoples.

Peaceful Settlement of International Disputes - Mediation and Conciliation
by Professor Andre Gros (France)

André Gros: b. 1908. Member, International Law Commission; 1947: Legal Adviser, French Ministry of Foreign Affairs; 1958 and 1960: Head of French Delegation, Conference on Law of the Sea, Geneva; Member of French Delegation to numerous international conferences, including UN General Assembly and Security Council; member, various international conciliation and arbitration commissions.

Our subject tonight, the peaceful settlement of international disputes, has to do with one of the gravest problems confronting statesmen in our time. At the outset, it will be as well to give some thought to the nature of the international world. In its traditional aspect, that world consists of a network of relationships between numerous sovereign and independent States. Diplomacy is a well-tried technique for carrying on their mutual relations and settling their disputes but, as we all know, it has not always been able to prevent their disputes from leading to war. In between these two forms of international dispute — those which diplomacy quietly settles and the great wars of history where it fails — there are many forms of international negotiation by which man has sought to avoid or settle disputes.

The means of settlement open to him have been of two kinds: juridical methods such as arbitration and judicial settlement, and methods of a non-juridicial or less juridical nature, for they cannot be too precisely distinguished. In this lecture, however, a distinction has to be made, because arbitration and judicial settlement are being dealt with by another speaker. This evening we are concerned with mediation and conciliation as what we must call "non-juridical" methods for the peaceful settlement of international disputes.

Let us first take another look at the international world and what it means. That world is by no means a simple thing for, in addition to the traditional sovereign States, it now includes many international organizations, of which this city of Geneva is an outstanding host. There are now, in fact, about one hundred such organizations, approximately as many as there are independent States in the world. Like the States, these organizations have now a recognized place in international law and within each of them the States members negotiate with one another by what amounts to a new kind of diplomacy.

Thus, in our time international relations are no longer merely relations between States, whether on the bilateral or the multilateral level. They exist also within a variety of important international organizations, each one of which has its own special area of competence. It follows from this that the alignments and mutual oppositions of States are not necessarily the same within all the various organizations to which they belong. In fact, the international world is much less stratified and much less rigid than the national. Economic, social and political changes are, of course, common in all countries and, to take one example, France has been through various significant changes in the past fifty years. Nevertheless, a sociologist would see an evolution, rather than a revolution, in the changing structure of France since 1910. But when we consider the changes which have taken place in the international world since that same year, we become conscious of an entirely new situation. The international world has not, however, developed equally fast or along the same lines everywhere. In the case of most countries' external dealings the network of relationships now varies from the very simple to the highly complex.

Switzerland, for example, in her dealings with Iceland will be virtually restricted to the purchase of fish; Switzerland and Iceland, we might say, maintain an elementary system of mutual relations as various States did in the 16th century. For an example of the more complex relations, we might take Switzerland, not just as an independent State but as a member of the Central Commission for Navigation of the Rhine: that oldest of international organizations, which was created as far back as 1815. The relations obtaining between members of the Rhine Commission are less elementary, but not yet really complex. Switzerland is a member of the Commission with other riparian States along the Rhine, as well as Belgium, the United States and the United Kingdom. Together these countries study technical and economic problems connected with Rhine navigation and take common decisions in the general interest.

Side by side with this still relatively simple form of organization across borders, there are now these entirely new, large-scale international organizations, reaching into every continent. They are, in effect, so many international worlds of their own. All the time, they are expressing their collective will in their spheres of authority, and this collective will is something different from the will of each of their States members. On occasions, it may be opposed to that of certain States, but the minority in such organizations usually has to accept decisions by the majority, as prescribed by the particular Charter of the organization concerned.

Three kinds of relationship thus obtain in the contemporary international world. Almost all modern States maintain with others direct and elementary relations, semi-organizational relations and relations involving membership of international organizations. The picture becomes still more complex when we realize that, within each country, there exists a whole series of secondary associations or groupings, sometimes of great importance. One thinks immediately of large scale business and financial enterprises having their own direct relations with similar organizations in other States. It follows that international disputes in a world like ours can arise from a multiplicity of causes wherever these varied interests clash, and that they tend to be more complex than purely political disagreements. Since each country is involved, either directly or through the activities of its nationals, in this varied network of international groupings, a dispute with another country may arise at any moment in connection with one of these national or sectional activities.

A recent example of such a dispute on the elementary level would be that between Iceland and the United Kingdom. Since Iceland depends upon her fisheries for ninety-five per cent of her earnings from exports, her fishing grounds are vital to her prosperity and foreign competition has led her to extend the territorial limits of the waters in which she claims exclusive rights for her fishermen. British fishermen, on the other hand, can no longer find near home the quantity of fish, which the British market needs and they have claimed the right to fish, as in the past, within three miles of Iceland's coastline, rejecting the Icelandic Government's newly imposed restrictions. The result was a clash of interests of a straightforward type such as has become familiar in the history of national States.

For an instance of a rather more complex type of dispute we can turn again to one of the simpler international organizations like the Rhine Commission. Let us suppose that one of the Member States of the Commission wants to carry goods not, as is usual, from one riparian State to another, but between two German cities on the Rhine. If the Federal Republic objected to this carrying trade by foreigners within its own territory, we should have an example of a more complex dispute calling for the legal interpretation of a single convention. The same country, Switzerland, can also give us an example of what we might call the complex type of international dispute. Switzerland is not a member of the European Economic Community (the Common Market), which has drawn up certain regulations concerning river transport and which proposes to apply these to the Rhine. As a non-member of the Community, Switzerland might well refuse to be bound by those regulations. If she did, we should have a complex dispute involving two international organizations and two agreements, one concerned with the Rhine only and one with Western European relations in a broader sphere.

The history of international disputes concerns the sociologist and the historian. It is the lawyer's task to seek means of settlement for such disputes when they occur. We do not always realize the importance of the rather discreet part which the lawyers play in this process, for many international disputes never reach the stage of becoming a serious threat to peace. Every day, without the knowledge of the general public, quite important disputes are being quietly settled. These are not always direct disputes between governments nor are they necessarily the subject of political debate in the countries concerned. Again, an example will make the point clearer. When one country negotiates with another to sign an aviation agreement, this may have considerable importance for its national aviation interests and even for its economic life as a whole, yet such an agreement will probably rate no more than a paragraph or two in the Press. It would, however, be true to say that there was probably an international conflict of interests before the negotiations opened. A solution has, nevertheless, been found at the technical level. If we compare with such a case the publicity given to disputes involving national independence, we shall see how publicity tends to inflame opinion, rather than to promote a settlement. If public opinion is not aware of, or not interested by, a dispute on the international level, that dispute will often be infinitely easier to settle. Before we look for solutions, it is therefore wise to aim, if possible, at securing a period of calm or a breathing space which only the political wisdom of governments can provide.

There is one — and only one — time-honoured formula for settling disputes — talking the problem over. But there are two non-juridical ways by which countries can set about doing this.

The first method is direct negotiation with the other party to the dispute; the second is to seek the assistance of a third party, who plays the role of an intermediary in a private quarrel. This intervention by a third party may take various forms, which are described by the terms good offices, mediation, inquiry and conciliation.

The method of direct negotiation, despite its greater complexity in our time, is fundamentally the same as in the far-off days when one chieftain would meet another to argue over hunting or fishing rights. Age-long experience shows that even strong clashes of interest can usually be solved by discussion, especially since the great majority of disputes are relatively simple and offer no real pretext for hostilities. For every dispute which becomes known to the general public, probably ten have been settled by the quiet intervention of diplomats and government legal advisers. Direct negotiation is the commonest means for settling such disputes and, thanks to its influence, the daily rhythm of international life is very much more peaceful than would seem to be the case from a reading of headlines.

One recent example of a political dispute which ended happily concerned the Antarctic. In November 1959, several countries sent representatives to Washington, where they discussed a number of conflicting territorial claims which they maintained in the Antarctic. Although territorial questions have usually proved the most difficult to solve and the most likely to lead to fighting, three weeks of discussion in Washington resulted in an agreement to establish an international regime for Antarctica.

The second "non-juridical" method for the peaceful settlement of disputes involves the intervention of a third party. In most cases, negotiations first begin directly between the two sides but, if they break down or run into difficulties, a third party may be called in to set the wheels turning again. This third party may do no more than help to restart negotiations, as it is often easier to accept the suggestions of a third party than to utter a *mea culpa*. It may, in some cases, be necessary for the third party to go further than this and actually to tell one of the opponents that he is in the wrong, from the legal point of view. Even in the so-called political settlement of international disputes, the legal angle is usually present and the lawyer's counsel is often sought.

This will be true of all the various methods of settlement by political or "non-legal" means — good offices, mediation, conciliation and, though in a lesser degree, inquiry or investigation. Let us glance at each of these in turn.

Good offices involve the intervention of a State not concerned in a dispute, which endeavours merely to bring the parties together without going so far as to propose a definite solution.

At the end of the last war, Thailand was involved in a frontier dispute with France which concerned not France directly, but two countries, Laos and Cambodia, for which France had an international responsibility. Recourse was had to the good offices of the United Kingdom and the United States, who brought the two parties together and helped them to negotiate a solution, without themselves proposing what that solution should be. More recent examples of good offices were to be seen in 1947 when the United States performed this service for Indonesia and the Netherlands, in 1951 when Burma and Indonesia assisted India and Pakistan in the Kashmir question and in 1958 when the United States undertook a similar mission for France and Tunisia.

The second method of "non-juridical" settlement is mediation. In this case, a third party, acting either upon request or spontaneously, intervenes in a dispute and suggests a solution to the two parties, a solution which, it goes without saying, they are not obliged to accept.

Mediation was regularized by the first Hague Convention of 1899 and by the Inter-American Convention of 1936, and it has been successfully practised by the United Nations, as when Count Folke Bernadotte was sent to Palestine and later replaced by Dr. Ralph Bunche, and when the Security Council appointed first Sir Owen Dixon and then the American Senator Mr. Frank Graham as mediator on the Kashmir question. As in the case of good offices, mediation efforts sometimes succeed and sometimes fail. Their value depends on circumstances.

An example of successful mediation was that by France in 1890 which led to the signing of the Treaty of Paris and so ended a war between the United States and Spain. An instance of failure would be India's rejection of Australia's offer to mediate in 1951 in the Kashmir dispute with Pakistan. By way of footnote, we may remark that the United States delegation at the Hague Peace Conference attached great weight to the method of bilateral mediation, by which two States involved in a dispute each nominate one other to meet and examine the problem *à deux*. This looks like an unconscious heritage from the technique of the duel. Despite its formal recognition in the Hague Convention, it has never been applied in practice.

The third "non-juridical" method of settlement is the inquiry carried out by an impartial commission. This idea was put forward by Russia at the Hague Peace Conference of 1899 and regularized by the second Conference, and Russia proved to be the first country to have recourse to such a commission of inquiry in the dispute over the British trawlers in 1904. Commissions of inquiry investigate the circumstances in which a given incident took place, but their role is limited to establishing the facts. They are not asked to draw conclusions or to assign responsibilities. However, in most cases, the facts themselves are eloquent. And, as we saw before, the views of the international lawyers may have something to contribute even to an inquiry into the true story of a historical incident.

Three times, in 1935, 1936 and 1938, the Negus sought in vain to have a commission of inquiry appointed by the League of Nations to discuss Ethiopia's dispute with Italy. In 1948, after a serious aerial incident near Berlin, a commission of inquiry was set up, from which the Soviet representative withdrew. In 1952, following the destruction of a Swedish seaplane off the island of Dagö, the USSR refused a commission of inquiry. On the brighter side of this particular balance sheet, let us recall that commissions of inquiry have been used to good effect by the United Nations in Greece, in Indonesia and in Palestine.

The last "non-juridical" method for the settlement of disputes is conciliation. This is the technique by which disputes are referred to a commission, generally consisting of five members of whom three are chosen from among the citizens of third party States, to ensure a "neutral" majority. Conciliation commissions may be set up on a permanent basis to smooth relations between States or on an *ad hoc* basic to deal with particular disputes. Quite recently, France has been a party to four disputes which were handled in this way. A conciliation commission with Thailand was set up following the agreement with that country which resulted from the use of good offices we noted earlier. Two French disputes with Switzerland and one with Morocco were also referred to conciliation commissions. One of the problems at issue with Switzerland concerned the Second World War. In 1940 certain elements of the French Army found themselves driven against the Swiss frontier by the German advance. They included a Polish Division formed of Poles in France by the Polish refugee Government. To avoid being taken prisoner, both French and Polish troops had to pass into Switzerland where they were interned for the rest of the war, enjoying the hospitality of the Swiss Government. The latter eventually asked the French Government to reimburse the expenses it had incurred both on behalf of the French and the Polish troops. By mutual agreement, the matter was referred to the Permanent Conciliation Commission between France and Switzerland, which met at The Hague, studied the written statements by both parties and heard oral statements by French and Swiss representatives. In all, the Commission held thirty-four meetings, at eight of which French and Swiss representatives were present. As conciliation is not a judicial method for settling disputes the Commission was not expected to decide the rights and wrongs of the case, but merely to break the deadlock in which the two parties found themselves. After long deliberations, the Commission stated its views on the problem without prejudice to the legal position of either party. Both France and Switzerland accepted those views and the dispute was settled.

By a similar procedure, conciliation has recently put an end to disputes between Belgium and Denmark and between Italy and Greece, but it would be wrong to conclude that it is any more effective than the other methods we have discussed. There is no magic cure for international disputes, but there is a choice of valuable methods for carrying on negotiation either directly or through a third party and it is the duty of governments to apply one or other method in good faith, and a fundamental principle of international law in all circumstances.

We have glanced very briefly at some of the possibilities available for settling international disputes without recourse to a judicial body. It is important to mention one other such possibility. We spoke of the many international organizations which now share the world scene with the traditional sovereign States. In our time, many international disputes are settled by these organizations themselves or as a result of their activities and this aspect of the question has become so important that it calls for treatment on its own. Solutions for serious political disputes are continually being sought in the United Nations itself, while in economic, financial and technical disagreements between States the specialized agencies have a very important role to play. An increasing use of the means for settlement we have been discussing and their application within the framework of the international organizations should lead gradually towards a limitation of international disputes and perhaps to their ultimate elimination.

The International Court of Justice and the Judicial Settlement of International Disputes
by Professor Jimenez de Aréchaga (Uruguay)

Eduardo Jimenez de Aréchaga: b. 1918. Member, International Law Commission; Professor of Public International Law, University of Montevideo; former Under-Secretary of State for Foreign Affairs (Uruguay); Secretary, National Council, Government of Uruguay; member, Uruguayan Delegation, Third and Fifth Sessions, United Nations General Assembly.

The Statute of the Permanent Court of International Justice was adopted in Geneva on 16 December 1920 and entered into force the following year. In 1945 at the San Francisco Conference it was decided to dissolve the Permanent Court and to set up what was technically a new Court with a new Statute. However, there was general agreement as to the substantial identity of these two organs. The present Statute is based on that adopted in 1920, even to the numbering of the articles, and there was no breach of continuity in the legal sense. The present Court is in substance a continuation of the older body. The name was altered because it was thought that to speak of a Permanent Court was redundant, and that the adjective "international" should apply to the organ and not to the justice administered by it.

During the past 40 years, the Court has shown that it marks a step forward from the arbitration tribunals which were previously the only legal organs providing for impartial third party settlement of disputes. Arbitration tribunals are generally born out of a specific conflict and disappear with its settlement. The Court, on the other hand, is a standing institution. In settling particular disputes, it restates and defines the pertinent rules of international law. Thus it has become a very important agent for the progressive restatement and development of international law. Its very continuity gives just that additional confidence which is so important in the present fragmentary state of international law. It thus becomes possible in many cases to anticipate and to predict what might be the answer of the Court to various legal questions arising in the relations between States.

The Court's Jurisdiction

When an individual is summoned to appear before a competent municipal tribunal, he is under a liability to do so. If he does not, the court may pass judgement on the case without hearing what he has to say in his own defence. This is the result of a long process of evolution, and the same point has not yet been reached in international law.

The International Court can exercise jurisdiction only if both States parties to a dispute give their consent. In other cases, the Court must refuse to try the dispute.

Consent may be given by both States either after a dispute has arisen or earlier, for instance, by means of a treaty such as the Pact of Bogotá, providing for the judicial settlement of all disputes or of certain types of dispute between States signing the treaty. Some treaties, like the Japanese Peace Treaty, contain a final clause to the effect that any disagreement regarding interpretation or application will be referred to the Court. Or again, this provision may be made the subject of an independent protocol, as was done at the Geneva Conference on the Law of the Sea and in the Vienna Convention on Diplomatic Intercourse and Immunities. Finally, States may consent to jurisdiction by the Court by subscribing to what is traditionally called the "optional clause."

The Optional Clause

When the Statute of the Permanent Court was drafted in 1920, a Commission of Jurists proposed to give the Court compulsory jurisdiction in all legal disputes, similar to that possessed by national courts. The Council of the League of Nations took a different view and was in favour of making the Court's jurisdiction voluntary. Agreement was finally reached on a compromise formula proposed by the Brazilian jurist, Raul Fernandez. This formula consists in what is generally called the "optional clause", otherwise Article 36, paragraph 2 of the Court's Statute.

Paragraph 1 of that Article states the basic principle of voluntary jurisdiction. Paragraph 2 adds that States parties to the Statute "may at any time declare that they recognize as compulsory *ipso facto* and without special agreement, in relation to any other State accepting the same obligation, the jurisdiction of the Court in all legal disputes".

A former President of the Court, Lord McNair, in his historic opinion on the Anglo-Iranian oil case (an important instance of a judge voting against the contention of his own State), described the system as follows:

"Under the Covenant of the League of Nations and the Statute of the Permanent Court of International Justice no State was under any obligation to accept the jurisdiction of that Court. However article 36 (2) of the Statute afforded to States such an opportunity of doing so by means of a voluntary act. That paragraph (which is reproduced in the Statute of the present Court in terms which are identical in all material respects) was in the nature of a standing invitation made on behalf of the Court to Members of the League of Nations to accept as compulsory, on the basis of reciprocity, the whole or any part of the jurisdiction of the Court as therein defined. It should be noted that the machinery provided by that paragraph is that of contracting in, not of contracting out."

There are now 39 States which have made this declaration, the first in date being my own country Uruguay, which became a party to the Statute as early as 1921. Among great powers which have made the declaration we have the United Kingdom, France and the United States — though, in this case, with serious reservations. European States include Belgium, Denmark, Finland, the Netherlands, Norway, Portugal, Sweden, Switzerland and Turkey. Australia, Canada, New Zealand and the Union of South Africa have made the declaration, as have Asian countries such as Cambodia, the Republic of China, India, Japan, Pakistan, the Philippines and Thailand together with ten Latin American

States. More recently, they have been followed by Israel and the Sudan.

Compulsory Jurisdiction

Although the Court's jurisdiction must always be based on the consent of the States parties, there is a distinction between compulsory and voluntary jurisdiction. According to the Statute, compulsory jurisdiction might seem to be restricted to the so-called optional clause and the declarations made in connexion with it. However, the prevailing legal opinion is that compulsory jurisdiction also comes into play when reference to the Court is provided for in treaties and conventions under paragraph 1 of Article 36. It has become a fine point of doctrine among international lawyers to determine the exact test for the concept of compulsory jurisdiction.

In former periods, if the Court was seized of a dispute between the two parties, it was considered that there was voluntary jurisdiction, by means of a special agreement. Unilateral arraignment of a State before the Court was considered appropriate only when compulsory jurisdiction existed. This test, however, no longer applied once the Court had ruled — in the Corfu Channel case — that unilateral arraignment was admissible even when compulsory jurisdiction did not exist.

Conversely, even when compulsory jurisdiction exists between the parties to a dispute, they may choose to seize the Court of it by means of a special agreement, as France and the United Kingdom did in the Channel Islands case or Belgium and the Netherlands in their dispute concerning certain frontier zones.

The distinguished British lawyer, Sir Gerald Fitzmaurice, now a member of the Court, proposed to take into account, when defining compulsory jurisdiction, the manner in which consent is given by a State, i.e. whether in advance of the dispute itself or of its reference to the Court (*ante hoc*), at the moment of its reference to the Court (*ad hoc*) or after reference to the Court (*post hoc* or *forum pro rogatum*).

Sir Gerald implies that compulsory jurisdiction would exist whenever consent has been given *ante hoc*, but he does not make it clear whether this consent should be given before the dispute or before its reference to the Court. The first interpretation would not seem to hold good. For instance, in 1948 the American States signing the Bogotá Pact accepting compulsory jurisdiction made it apply to pre-existing disputes, of which at least one dated back to the 19th century. Therefore, compulsory jurisdiction may be established even after a specific dispute occurs.

If, however, Sir Gerald has in mind the moment of reference to the Court, this could also lead to a wrong conclusion. In an important contribution to the literature of the subject, Professor Briggs has pointed out that, whenever two States enter into a special agreement for referring a specific dispute to the Court, this would be a commitment prior to submission. Therefore, if Sir Gerald's criterion were applicable, it would also constitute compulsory jurisdiction and we would no longer have any voluntary jurisdiction at all.

Professor Briggs himself proposes that, if the commitment refers to a specific dispute, there is voluntary and not compulsory jurisdiction, whereas, if the undertaking is general in nature and does not refer to a particular case, there is compulsory jurisdiction.

With all due respect, I am not entirely convinced by Professor Briggs' argument. Two States might enter into an agreement relating to a specific dispute such as a boundary question and might undertake to refer such a question to the Court, if other methods failed. To my mind, when eventual reference to the Court takes place under this agreement, we still have compulsory and not voluntary jurisdiction. As a practical criterion or rule of thumb to determine when compulsory jurisdiction exists, I may suggest, borrowing Professor Briggs' words, that it is present "whenever the *ad hoc* consent of the respondent State to the exercise of jurisdiction in a specific case is irrelevant". In other words, compulsory jurisdiction exists whenever the Court is empowered to exercise its jurisdiction even if the respondent State does not appear at the Bar, and when Article 53 of the Statute, on Procedure by Default, becomes applicable. The idea of compulsory jurisdiction is thus linked with its traditional meaning in civil procedure; a liability for the respondent to appear and defend his case with the understanding that, if he does not do so, judgement will be passed, anyway.

Terms, Conditions and Reservations of the Optional Clause

According to paragraph 3 of Article 36, declarations of acceptance of compulsory jurisdiction by the Court may be made unconditionally, or on condition of reciprocity on the part of several or certain States, or for a certain time. The Statute does not mention the most important of the restrictions to which these declarations are subject, and the one which most seriously affects the efficiency of the system: that of reservations. As Lord McNair pointed out in his separate opinion already referred to, a State, being free either to make a declaration or not, is entitled to limit the scope of its declaration in any way it chooses.

States have, in fact, made such widespread use of their power to enter reservations that this tendency threatens to disintegrate the minimum of compromise which is embodied in the optional clause.

One reservation introduced by the United States, and later copied by other countries such as France, India, Liberia, Mexico, Pakistan and the Union of South Africa, is open to very serious doubts on grounds of legality. I refer to the so-called Connally Amendment or the automatic reservation of domestic matters "as determined by the reserving State". The Court has not yet passed upon the legality of this reservation, having taken great pains to avoid a decision on the issue, but various influential members of the Court have declared their opinion that this reservation is not legally valid. A basic argument is that the automatic reservation violates Article 36, paragraph 6, of the Statute, according to which "in the event of a dispute as to whether the Court has jurisdiction, the matter shall be settled by the decision of the Court." This statutory power of the Court to determine its own jurisdiction *(compétence de la compétence)* cannot be subject to reservations by one of the parties acting at its own discretion. It has been pointed out that the automatic reservation is contrary to the Statute of the Court and that it denies acceptance of the indispensable element of legal obligation.

Bilateral Effects of Reservations

Every reservation by a State benefits the other State party to the specific dispute at issue. For instance, in the case of the loans between Norway and France, Norway, relying on the automatic reservation made by France, interpreted the matter as one belonging to her domestic jurisdiction. As Lord McNair put it, "another State seeking to found the jurisdiction of the Court on the optional clause system, must show that the declarations of both States concur in comprising the dispute in question within their scope." This bilateral effect might be a strong incentive for States to drop the automatic reservation, because they could rarely compel any other State to come before the Court. A good sign is that in 1959 and 1960 France, India and Pakistan withdrew the automatic reservation.

The Record of the Court

In spite of all these difficulties, the Court has an impressive record covering the last 40 years. Already, 33 international cases have been solved by judicial settlement. If we deduct the seven years in which the Court was inactive because of the war, we have an average of one dispute a year decided on its merits. Some of these cases referred to important disputes and were also of significance because of the legal principles involved and established in the Court's decisions.

Let us recall a few of these cases. There were the decisions on the Free Zone of Haute Savoie and Gex, of great importance in connexion with the law of treaties; on the territorial jurisdiction of the River Oder, where basic principles of river law were established; on the legal status of Eastern Greenland, important in connexion with problems of sovereignty over Arctic and Polar regions; on the case of the *Société Commerciale de Belgique*, of primary importance in the question of arbitration between States and private companies.

All these were decisions reached by the former Permanent Court. Let us mention a few which we owe to the International Court. There were the asylum case and its sequel the Haya de la Torre case, which disposed of a serious dispute between two Latin American countries; the Anglo-Norwegian Fisheries case, which established basic principles on the territorial sea, later incorporated in the Geneva Convention on the subject; the rights of United States nationals in Morocco, of interest for establishing the legal status of Protectorates as subjects of international law; the Channel Islands case between France and the United Kingdom, where basic principles in connexion with the acquisition of territorial sovereignty of islands and the law of prescription were established or agreed by the agents of the parties; the Nottebohm case, of primary importance on the law of nationality; the decision on right of passage over Indian territory, whose legal implications may assist in solving international problems of the utmost political significance in our time; and the Court's last decision on the validity of the arbitration award of the King of Spain between Honduras and Nicaragua.

Some of these disputes were serious enough to engage the attention of the political organs of the United Nations, as did the Corfu Channel case, considered by the Security Council in 1947. The frontier case between Honduras and Nicaragua had to be called to the attention of the Council of the Organization of American States, acting under the Treaty of Rio de Janeiro.

There is a striking resemblance between the co-ordinated international action of these political organs and of the Court and the way in which justice was organized under ancient Roman law, in the transitional stage from private to public justice. Before the public authority assumed its full judicial functions in Rome, the *praetor* was called upon to prevent a solution by force among the disputants and to conduct them to a private *judex*, who was invited to settle the substance of the question. In the two international cases cited above, there were the same successive stages. First, a political organ prevented the parties from seeking a solution by force and referred them to the Court. Later the Court passed on the merits of the case.

We can thus console ourselves with the thought that the international community in our time is slowly retracing the steps followed by national communities to settle differences among their citizens, but we may well ask whether we have the time and the patience to do internationally what individual States slowly succeeded in doing. As Professor Brierly has pointed out, we are faced by the paradoxical situation that we have a primitive legal system attempting to regulate the complex relations between States that are in a more advanced technological stage than the world has ever known. In fact, our international community is primitive only in the one rather fundamental matter of its legal organization.

Advisory Procedure

I wish to add a few words in connexion with one special function of the Court, its power to give advisory opinions on any legal question at the request of the General Assembly, the Security Council or other organs of the United Nations and specialized agencies so authorized by the General Assembly.

This power of a Court to act as adviser on legal questions is held by the Judiciary Committee of the British Privy Council and it was granted to the Permanent Court as the result of a British proposal.

As Professor Gros explained to us the other day, most disputes, even of a predominantly political nature, have many legal aspects and it is often of great assistance in advancing to a settlement through negotiation or concilation, when an advisory opinion of the Court is available on these legal aspects. Because of the Court's prestige and authority and because of the quasi-judicial method followed in its deliberations, such opinions have provided a convenient basis for further negotiations and for the eventual settlement of disputes, even when those disputes were not, as a whole, apt for judicial settlement.

An example would be the well-known advisory opinion of the Permanent Court on the nationality decrees in Tunisia and Morocco, which was instrumental in settling a controversy between France and the United Kingdom. The International Court gave an advisory opinion on the legal entity of the United Nations and its power to claim indemnities from States. This opinion had considerable legal significance in relation to the international organizations, and it also helped in the settlement of specific disputes between the State of Israel and other claimants.

The Court has ruled that the power to give an opinion on any legal question, granted to it in Article 96 of the Charter of the United Nations, covers current questions at issue between two or more States, but, as it declared on one such occasion, those opinions are not binding. "It follows that no State can prevent the giving of an advisory opinion which the United Nations considers to be desirable, in order to obtain enlightenment as to the course of action it should take. The Court opinion is given not to the States but to the organ which is entitled to request it; the reply of the Court, itself an organ of the United Nations, represents its participation in the activities of the Organization and, in principle, should not be refused."

The Importance of International Law in the Maintenance of Peace
by Arthur H. Dean (USA)

Arthur H. Dean: b. 1898. 1962: Head of United States Delegation, Eighteen Nation Committee on Disarmament; 1958 and 1960: Chairman, United States Delegation, Conferences on the Law of the Sea, Geneva; 1954: Special Ambassador to Republic of Korea; 1953: represented US and 16 other nations contributing UN troops in the post-armistice negotiations at Panmunjom, Korea; Member of the Executive Council of the American Society of International Law. Mr. Dean's lecture was given in his private capacity.

If there is to be progress in law, there must be some acceptance of common principle, and thus the first exponents of the law in Europe were the canon lawyers of the Western Church. They were concerned with what we now call Western Europe, and they did not waste their time drawing up rules for those who were not likely to accept their authority. Grotius, following in the footsteps of his medieval predecessors, assumed that the hundreds of independent rulers in Western Europe might agree to accept a common body of legal rules based on the Christian religion, which they all professed, and on the Roman jurisprudence, rules which could express agreed moral principles in terms of positive law.

In our time, the common cultural unity upon which the law was originally founded has been destroyed in its own original home, that is to say, in Europe.

The Expanding Scope of International Law

Traditionally, international law governs only the relationship between States, but in practice it is coming to include many of the problems faced by private citizens or business enterprise. Private disputes between citizens may come to influence the foreign policy of the States concerned, since the prestige of the sovereign State may be involved in what is essentially a private dispute. Unfortunately, political factors often prevent the settlement of such disputes in national courts, and the frequent absence of any clear agreement on principles of law which can be applied across national boundaries impedes mutual confidence.

Only infrequently does one government adopt rules which others will follow, as all nations came to follow the maritime rules of the road enacted by Great Britain in the Merchant Shipping Amendment Act of 1862 and the Merchant Shipping Acts of 1873 and 1874. Yet, the need is great in many areas of law, as studies of various conflicts of law in different countries have shown. The tendency to politicize such subjects as law and commerce adds to the difficulties of joint action and codification. There should be continuing efforts to develop reasonable rules which will govern the myriad problems of private and commercial relations across national boundaries. Unless there is a broad basis of understanding, law cannot function.

The future of international law is closely connected with the future of international organizations, which have been instrumental in developing much public international law and applying it, and recent changes in the traditional concept of international law are nowhere more clearly to be seen than in connexion with the specialized agencies related to the United Nations.

The Contemporary Social and Political Context of International Law

The subject matter, complexity and importance of disputes which should be made internationally justiciable, in whole or in part, have greatly increased in recent years. The increase in international capital movements and trade, extensive changes in the forms of political and social organization, the birth of new nations, various factors which make the economies of the world increasingly interdependent and new technological developments have combined to cause a steadily increasing need for international law. Meanwhile, new destructive weapons have magnified the danger of each failure to settle international disputes to a point where most nations are aware of the cumulative menace.

In our contemporary world, the "vital interests" of almost every nation, and not merely of the most powerful, have expanded and are expanding beyond their national territory to every corner of the globe. As an example of the interdependence of that world, in a period of continual change such as ours, it may be observed that the recognition or non-recognition of governments, and the propriety and type of support furnished or allegedly furnished by the major powers on behalf of one political faction or another, have become legal and international problems of fundamental importance. In recent years, the standards and distinctions relating to recognition of revolutionary movements, and to rights and duties with respect to them, have not undergone any notable clarification, nor have they been the subject of an increasing consensus of views. Indeed, the opposite seems true, in spite of the importance of such standards in current controversies.

Wherever there is such a failure to clarify rules respecting important current situations, international law tends to lose touch with reality. Legal concepts may have to be changed or developed to deal adequately with the full contemporary scope of problems such as state succession, self-determination, non-intervention, international responsibility, sovereignty and the legal and juridical role of the United Nations, especially when it is operating in countries to preserve law and order. The new nations are vitally concerned with the strengthening of international law standards in the fields of peace, neutrality and security, investment and technical assistance.

Achieving Full Acceptance of the Rule of Law

One of the keys to ensure the growth of a body of international law adequate to meet current problems is the finding of ways to bring justiciable disputes before the International Court of Justice.

The process of inducing States to increase the number and importance of the truly legal issues that they will agree to consider justiciable is a matter requiring both internal political action and diplomatic negotiation. Public opinion — or the makers of public opinion — must be induced to support, or at least not to obstruct, the process and to accept and agree to live by the results. No real progress will be made until the true compulsory jurisdiction of the International Court can be achieved, both by increasing the number of countries which accept it and by eliminating reservations from existing declarations on the subject. It may be noted that the leading American Bar Associations in the United States are conducting an intensive campaign, supported by both former President Eisenhower and President Kennedy, to eliminate the specific United States reservation known as the Connally Amendment.

States may decide against unreserved acceptance of compulsory jurisdiction for a variety of reasons. These include national sensitivity, pride and fear for national security and the whole question of trust in the objective fairness of others. On a purely legal plane, it is sometimes argued that acceptance of compulsory jurisdiction must be contingent upon clarification of the international law which the Court is supposed to apply. However, much of this objection proves to be simply a rationalization for unexpressed fears and for the mistrust of non-nationals designated as neutral or impartial and purporting to act in an objective capacity.

Fear of adverse public opinion in the event of a decision against the national interest may be one reason why fewer than half the members of the United Nations have accepted compulsory jurisdiction by the Court, without more or less serious reservations. No member of the Soviet bloc has so far announced its willingness to accept such jurisdiction.

Among influences which may exert increasing pressure for the unreserved acceptance of compulsory jurisdiction, is the growing domestic and international prestige attaching to a State which conducts its affairs under established principles of international law rather than by the use of naked power. Many smaller States, which are unwilling to align themselves politically with larger States, may be disposed to join others in a "law bloc" which bases its conduct primarily on respect for law and only secondarily on the political advantage of the moment.

As the United Nations grows in membership and serves more frequently for the full discussion of international disputes, the non-judicial judgements of the General Assembly may come, in time, to be authoritative, quasi-legislative pronouncements on an increasing range of topics not covered by Article 2, paragraph 7 of the Charter, which excludes matters "essentially within the domestic jurisdiction of any State". Since it appears increasingly likely that the conduct of sovereign States will be judged by an outside body in one form or another, it seems essential that, in legal disputes, the decisions of the Court should be available as alternative, or as clarifying preliminaries, to the non-legal or quasi-legal judgements of the General Assembly. Such decisions of the Court are arrived at under carefully enunciated safeguards of legal procedure and without the emotional overtones and bloc voting sometimes associated with General Assembly debates.

Is There a Need to Codify International Law?

The patient codification and progressive development of many areas of public international law through agreements between as many nations as possible appears to be an immediate and desirable goal. States have been moving towards this goal with increasing degrees of success, notwithstanding temporary setbacks.

The earliest sources of international law doctrine were, by and large, Western writers, regarded as authoritative, who attempted to express the general consensus of opinion and practice, almost all of which was derived from the Greco-Roman heritage of Europe. There also came to be a growing body of bilateral and regional treaties which directly codified law for the parties concerned and were used to settle questions, particularly those relating to war and the conclusion of hostilities. The more extensive attempts at codification in the 19th century resulted from an effort by large segments of the international community to plan for the future, rather than to rely on ad hoc adjustments of particular events. However, many of these efforts were still limited to dealing with wars and other international emergencies. Since the creation of the League of Nations in 1919, there have been much more extensive attempts to deal with the peacetime problems and normal relations of the international community.

While the increasing loss of any sense of fundamental moral and religious unity in the world has undermined the authority of traditional law, in general, many conventions have been adopted which reflect a general consensus of States in various areas of economic and social relations previously considered to be solely within the national domain. The increasing tempo of this convention-drafting was directly connected with the growing volume and complexity of international commerce and the growth of technology. By the 1930's international conventions had codified rules respecting civil aviation, radio broadcasting, postal communications, telegraphy, weights and measures, copyright and a variety of other subjects. In 1958 and 1960, the first such conferences called by the United Nations on the Law of the Sea resulted in large areas of agreement and in significant compromises acceptable to the great majority of nations. These agreements were in large measure based upon draft articles proposed by the International Law Commission.

The Vienna United Nations Conference on Diplomatic Intercourse and Immunities held in 1961 adopted a Convention on Diplomatic Relations. It can only be hoped that the series of conferences now envisaged following recommendations by the International Law Commission will continue to clarify and adopt principles of law which nations will respect and will permit courts to apply. In the midst of cold war tensions, notable success was achieved in 1960 with respect to Antarctica, a matter of lasting importance to the international community. This treaty is a great tribute to the scholarship and patient attention to detail of my colleagues Herman Phleger of the United States and Professor Tunkin of the Soviet Union.

Looking at the history of past achievements, it is thus apparent that large segments of the international community have already agreed to codify the legal rules which are to govern their conduct in very substantial areas.

Needs of the Future: rules relating to contemporary problems of world commerce

Looking to the future, there is a clear need for agreements on international law relating to the complex problems of world commerce, transportation and the movement of bodies in the sensible atmosphere and in outer space, as well as on and under the sea. Economic plans to meet the crucial problems facing many of the new African and Asian States will be intimately affected by the stability of political life and the development of law in those States and in the international community. To ensure that all peoples can benefit from increased international trade, it is important that rules of law be established governing such trade and assuring businessmen of some acceptable measure of protection for their enterprises. For this purpose, new agreements are urgently needed. An important question which may arise in an economic development contract is what system of law shall be applied in the drafting and interpretation of the agreement. In such cases it may be highly desirable to apply some kind of international standard for the States and businessmen attempting to make such contracts.

Furthermore, the twilight areas between public and private international law must be explored, particularly where they have a direct bearing on economic development. Such development should lead to the greater well-being and stability of peoples and thus favour the firmer establishment of the rule of law.

Conclusion

The economic and technological areas at which we have glanced are only a fraction of a whole complex of international relations in which many disputes could be settled on a legal basis. If we fail to provide legal rules and processes wherever it is possible, we permit inequities which give rise to friction and resentment. This makes it more difficult to achieve agreements on other international problems, some of which are so critical that they threaten civilization.

The inadequacy of law and legal procedures may cause law itself to fall into disrepute as a means of adjusting differences and regulating conduct. Delay in preventing this will threaten the basic moral consensus on which the whole international order must be built. We must therefore set ourselves, with a real sense of urgency, to seek that international consensus of legally acceptable principles in all areas where reasonable men can agree, even though their agreement may involve some infringement of national sovereignty. We shall, however, do law a disservice if we contend that essentially political problems can be solved by legal means.

Maximum demands will undoubtedly be made on the moral authority and the facilities of the international organizations which have already been created. In the final analysis, however, the future development of international legal principles into coherent patterns will depend on the workmanlike attitude and persistent interest of international lawyers, acting not merely as nationals of particular countries, but following the broader patterns laid out for them by the scholars in universities, the International Law Commission and the various legal societies in the United States, Europe and other countries.

International Law and Peace
by Professor Grigori I. Tunkin (USSR)

Grigori I. Tunkin: b. 1906. Chairman, International Law Commission; Head of Legal and Treaties Department, Ministry of Foreign Affairs, USSR; 1961: Head of USSR Delegation, Conference on Diplomatic Intercourse and Immunities, Vienna; 1960 and 1958: Head of USSR Delegation, Conferences on the Law of the Sea, Geneva; 1948-1954; Professor of International Law, Moscow Institute of Law and Foreign Relations; President, Soviet Association of International Law.

My topic covers essentially two problems which in themselves are probably all-embracing. The first may be expressed as follows. What, in general, is the nature of contemporary international law considered from the point of view of the maintenance of international peace? In other words, can contemporary international law be considered to be an instrument of peace? The second problem concerns the specific impact of international law on international relations. These, in my opinion, are fundamental problems in an age which is witnessing great changes in human society.

In the twentieth century, a completely new social system has emerged based on common ownership of the means of production and a period of co-existence of two different economic systems has begun. Meanwhile, the colonial régime is in a state of complete disintegration, and we are witnessing unprecedented scientific and technical achievements, such as the release of atomic energy, and the exploration of outer space heralded by the flight of Yuri Gagarin. These technical achievements open new horizons before humanity, but at the same time they greatly increase the destructive power of weapons of war. Herein lies a real menace to human society.

In this situation, we have to admit that much confusion exists with regard to the problems I have indicated. The opinion has been expressed that international law lags far behind the existing international situation and that therefore it should be completely recast. Plans for such a reconstruction of international law have been drafted. In my opinion, they all suffer from a fundamental error. They are prepared on the assumption that international law should be framed according to the wishes of great statesmen or of great international lawyers. But this is not the case. The norms of international law are formed by agreement between States. One might say that the norms of international law express the co-ordinated wills of various States. In the final analysis, the development of international law is conditioned in its main features, by the laws which control the development of human society.

The wills of States (in a capitalist State this is, in fact, a will of a ruling class; in a socialist State, a will of the people) are determined by historical circumstances. It is useless, therefore, to seek to explain a specific feature or deficiency of present-day international law by referring to the ill-will of States or statesmen or to certain theories. We should rather try to find some link between the specific characteristics of international law and those fundamental laws of historical development which find expression in the facts of human society in general and in those relating to various international situations in particular.

Some of the specific characteristics of international law are well-known to everyone, the absence of a legislature, an executive power, a judiciary. There is no legislature able to impose the norms of international law upon the subjects of it. There is no, or almost no, executive power which can take the necessary measures for enforcement.

These specific features of international law are conditioned by the fact that human society today consists of independent States.

We have to remember that the State as a form of organization belongs only to a certain period of human history, the period when society is divided into classes. Before the State as a social institution appeared, there was a period of human history when there was no State organization. There was, indeed, another form of social organization, but there was no State and there was no law. The extinction of social classes which is inevitable at a high level of development of human society, would bring with it the extinction of the State as a social institution. This would not mean that there would then be no organization of human society. At that higher level of social development there would be a more perfect social organization. It would not, however, be the State. There would be also no law and therefore no international law, but there would certainly be rules of human conduct, as distinct from the rules of law.

We must bear in mind that this is still the period of history when the sovereign State is the accepted form of social organization. A particular feature of the present-day situation is that those sovereign States belong to one of two fundamentally different social systems. Thus, we are confronted by the co-existence of independent States, of States belonging to two opposing systems. Their peaceful existence is an urgent necessity; it is also a basis of contemporary international law.

Let us inquire what was the nature of international law before the First World War, before the Great October Socialist Revolution. What transformations have occurred during the period of the co-existence of two systems?

The old international law, in effect, sanctioned the rule of force in international relations. It recognized *jus ad bellum*. War was permitted as a relationship between States. International law sanctioned the new situation which might be created by such recourses to violence, although this new situation had no relation, either in fact or in law, to the causes of the war or to the claims advanced by the contending parties. It mattered little which party started the war. The only valid consideration was which State won the war. Having achieved victory by force of arms, it could impose peace conditions which might have nothing to do with the original situation that led to the war itself.

By way of contrast, contemporary international law prohibits the aggressive war, the use of force against the territorial integrity and political independence of any State. It prohibits even the threat of force. It is therefore directed against war. Once the recourse to war was prohibited, international law became a kind of instrument for maintaining peace. That was a great historical change.

The old international law recognized two equal states or conditions of international relations — peace and war. You will recall the famous work of Grotius entitled *"De Jure Belli ac Pacis"*. The law of war was put first and only after it came the law of peace. In fact, problems of the law of war constituted the major part of international law. I would remind you that of the fourteen documents signed at the Second Hague Peace Conference in 1907, only two dealt with peaceful relations among States. The rest of them — that is twelve documents — dealt with problems of war.

Contemporary international law starts from a very different premise. The state of war is no longer regarded as a normal state of relations between States. Contemporary international law does not recognize two equal situations or equal states — the state of war and the state of peace. A recourse to war is the greatest breach of modern international law, involving a grave responsibility on the part of the aggressor State and also the criminal responsibility of persons guilty of starting the war.

We may note with satisfaction that a high percentage of the international instruments elaborated during the last 15 years are dedicated to peaceful relations between States. I could cite many international conventions such as the Conventions on the Law of the Sea or the Convention on Diplomatic Relations recently adopted in Vienna and many other international instruments.

It should be recalled that the old international law was essentially colonial. It had been created mainly by colonial Powers and it contained norms and principles which were instrumental in establishing and maintaining colonial rule. Contemporary international law is in substance anti-colonial. It recognizes the principle of the self-determination of peoples, which means that the sovereignty of any State should be based not on the suppression of the right of peoples to self-determination, but on the realization of that right. With this recognition of the principle of the self-determination of peoples, contemporary international law became a means for the liberation of colonial peoples.

The old international law was a law primarily, as it was usually put, of civilized nations. Although in origin it was practically European international law, its field was subsequently enlarged. A major portion of the population of the globe was under colonial rule and did not take part in international relations. Even independent Asian and African States were not considered as the equals of European States. In our day, with the disintegration of the colonial system and the emergence on to the international arena of many new States, international law is reaching out towards universality. It is still not universal, there are still some obstacles — sometimes artificial obstacles — which prevent international law from becoming universal.

To cite one example of these artificial difficulties, we may take the Vienna Convention on Diplomatic Relations. There was much discussion in Vienna on the subject of accession to this Convention. Not all the States were represented there. Some of them were deliberately excluded from taking part in this Conference by applying a standard formula according to which only States Members of the United Nations and Members of the specialized agencies were invited. As regards the problem of accession to the Convention, there was very strong support given to the view that, as such a Convention was intended to create or codify the norms of general international law, it was in the interest of all countries that the greatest possible number of States should be parties to it. Acting upon the main principles of international law, how could we exclude some States from participation in a Convention which deals with the rules of that law? All States are interested in those rules, and according to the principle of the equality of States, we ought to have admitted all States to the Convention. There was, however, opposition to this obvious truth and the Conference adopted what was, from the legal point of view an absurd provision according to which only States Members of the United Nations and Members of the specialized agencies could accede to the Convention.

Such obstacles are artificial and harmful to the development of international law. Under the influence of forces striving to maintain and develop peaceful co-existence, international law has undergone great transformations. The international law of today is fundamentally different from the international law which existed prior to the period of the co-existence of two systems. This new international law might be called a law of peaceful co-existence because its principal new features have appeared as a result of peaceful co-existence of States belonging to two systems and it is now directed primarily to ensuring peaceful co-existence among all States and and specifically among the States belonging to two different social systems.

The strict observance of the principles and norms of international law by all States is, therefore, indispensable for ensuring peaceful co-existence. This relationship between international law and peaceful co-existence has been stressed by N. S. Khrushchev, Chairman of the Council of Ministers of the USSR, who stated that, without respect for the norms of international law, without the carrying out of obligations assumed in relations between States, there can be no confidence, and without confidence there cannot be peaceful co-existence (*Pravda*, 1 September 1959).

I pass now to the second problem with which I opened these remarks, namely the impact of international law upon international relations. We often hear the complaint that international law is ineffective. We also hear the view expressed that there is only one way open to us to make international law effective — the creation of a world State. We all know that this approach is unrealistic and, I would say, harmful to international law.

There is, also another view often expressed, according to which if not a world State, at least compulsory international jurisdiction, is indispensable to make international law effective. This, I would say, is a very fashionable concept among Western international lawyers. I think it is only what I might call a practising lawyer's argument. It views the effectiveness of international law from the standpoint of a practising lawyer who is accustomed to compulsory jurisdiction in domestic law and who transports this idea into the field of international law. But, international practice shows that to see in compulsory jurisdiction the best way to make international law effective is to take too narrow a view. Of course, this does not mean in any way that I deny the usefulness of the judicial settlement of international disputes or, indeed, any other peaceful means for the settlement of international controversies. Both views I have indicated are based on the assumption that the effectiveness of international law depends primarily, if not exclusively, on the possibility of applying compulsion. The possibility of applying State compulsion is one of the most important distinguishing features of law in general and of international law in particular. We must, however, bear in mind that the real influence of international law, and I would say of law in general, does not depend exclusively on the possibility of applying State compulsion. This concept assumes that international law develops in the same way as municipal law. But this is not the case. We have no reason whatsoever to conclude that the development of international law justifies such a conclusion. We should rather proceed from the quite different asssumption that international law is different in many very important respects from municipal law. We must approach international law as a phenomenon in its own right, as something distinct from municipal law.

If we accept this point of view we have to examine various possibilities of admittedly varying importance for strengthening international law. We may admit, and we must admit, that there are certain very considerable obstacles in our way, but, in spite of these, there are much greater possibilities of making international law more effective than it is now. These possibilities may be of a legal nature or not, they may be of major or minor importance. Negotiation and other means of peaceful settlement of international disputes, international conferences, international organizations and many other possibilities lie open to us for increasing the role of law in international relations.

We can also envisage the development of such important institutions as that of permanent neutrality. The Laos Conference is now sitting in Geneva. It is dealing with the problem of the peaceful settlement of the Laotian question. But what does this mean from the point of view of international law? All the parties, or almost all the parties, at this Conference have agreed that Laos should be neutral, that the institution of permanent neutrality should be applied to this case and used to settle this international problem. If this institution of permanent neutrality is indeed applied to this case, it will not only settle this not unimportant international problem, but will also be a very interesting example of the application of international law to the settlement of a specific international situation.

A possibility of paramount importance is the total disarmament proposed by the Soviet Union. Total disarmament is a wide road to peace. Its realisation would mean a considerable extension of international law to a new field of international relations which at present is covered by law quite inadequately. A complete disarmament would radically change the international situation and greatly reinforce the foundations of peaceful co-existence. One consequence would be an increase, and probably the greatest increase we can envisage, in the effectiveness of international law. We should not forget that disarmament is not only a political problem, it is also a legal one. Thus it is not only a problem for statesmen, but also a problem for lawyers to deal with.

The essential point to keep in mind is that the growth and activity of the social forces of peace will be decisive for the effectiveness of international law and for the maintenance of international peace. Happily, this growth of the forces of peace is not only something to be desired; it is also a fact. For this reason — and on this note I conclude — we may look forward with considerable confidence to the prospects of international law in our time.

The Birth of Autonomous International Law
by Professor Paul Guggenheim (Switzerland)

Paul Guggenheim: b.1899. 1955: Professor of Public International Law, University of Geneva; 1941: Professor of International Law, Institut Universitaire des Hautes Etudes Internationales, Geneva; Member, Institute of International Law and Permanent Court of Arbitration; ad hoc Judge, International Court of Justice, The Hague; President, World Federation of United Nations Associations.

My subject is the history of international law and I shall seek to show as succinctly as possible how contemporary international law has evolved as an autonomous legal system. International law was relatively late in winning recognition and, not so very long ago, its rules were indistinguishable from some of those belonging to national legal systems. A long historical process was necessary before these elements of national law concerned with international relations became the principles of an autonomous international law.

Let us first consider a point of terminology. When we speak of public international law, we are using an expression which is relatively new in the world. It was, in fact, introduced by Jeremy Bentham in the introduction to his book, published in 1789, on the principles of morality and legislation. For the first time on that occasion, he used the word "international" to describe the law applicable to the international community. Before Bentham, the favoured expression was the "law of nations", corresponding to the Roman *jus gentium*. This was the expression habitually used by lawyers to describe the principles governing the relations of countries and of their rulers. The great founders of public international law — Grotius, Pufendorf, Vattel — spoke of it as the law of nations.

Where did this law of nations come from? The notion of *jus gentium* is first met with in Roman law, where it referred to the special legal status granted to foreigners in Rome who were not subject to the Roman civil law that applied exclusively to Roman citizens. Since foreigners were not included in the provisions of ordinary civil law, some means had to be found to deal with legal disputes in which they might become involved, either with Roman citizens or with other foreigners. The *jus gentium* could thus come into play without its being suggested that there was a legal system in Rome which was above the national law. In classical times, the *jus gentium,* as applied to foreigners, was therefore merely a part of ordinary Roman law, devised for a special purpose.

Neverthelesss, it held a germ for the future. *Jus gentium* was the first instance on record of a legal relationship which embraced all men, including foreigners, in a community designed to help them. This idea found expression in a famous comment by the Roman jurist Gaius, who said that the *jus gentium* was an expression of the natural reason inherent in all men, and not only in Roman citizens. The Romans, however, were a realistic people and they favoured pragmatic solutions. Their system of law had little to do with non-juridical or ideological concepts. The notion of a law of nations appealed to them because it offered a form of legal protection to those foreigners who stood outside the benefits of Roman law and, during the classical period of Roman law, jurists did no more than establish a distinction between the *jus civile* and the *jus gentium.*

In the compilation of Justinian, there appears for the first time the famous tripartite concept of civil law, law of nations and law of nature. At first the jurists did not perceive much difference between the law of nations and what they called the law of nature, which was a concept tending to put men into one category as human beings. The concept of a law of nations had always included some trace of this idea, because of its being associated with the gift of reason shared by all men. According to the jurist Ulpian, the difference between the law of nature and the law of nations could be illustrated by the fact that slavery, while conformable to the law of nations, was contrary to that of nature.

The triple distinction between civil law, the law of nations and the law of nature assumed its real importance only when the mediaeval Christian theologians began to erect their structure of ecclesiastical or canon law. Their object was to lay down Christian principles by which communities could live, as they had formally done by accepting the common law of Rome. These Christian lawgivers based on their efforts partly on the Apostle Paul's *Epistle to the Romans*, in which he had declared that the Gentiles, although they had not the privilege of the Law of Moses, nevertheless had a law written in their hearts, which taught them to distinguish between good and evil, and by which they would be judged at the last day. Unlike Roman law, this concept of a law of nature allowed for the existence of a higher authority than man and his legal systems.

While for a Roman jurist the law of nations had its basis in Roman national law, the Church Fathers saw in the law of nature an element making for unity among men and deriving ultimately from the picture of man as God's image. This concept was explicitly stated by St. Isidore, a sixth century Bishop of Seville, in the fifth book of his *Etymologies* — where he defined the law of nature as being a factor common to all nations, whose origin was to be sought in the natural instincts of man and not in any human legislative system. Two centuries before Isidore, St. Augustine had drawn an important conclusion from the rivalry which had begun to assert itself between the law of nature and Roman law. For Augustine, law eternal (law of nature) takes precedence over temporal and secular law.

How does the law of nations fit into the tripartite system we have been considering — law of nature, law of nations, civil law? St. Isidore of Seville defined the law of nations in the sixth century as a man-made law and therefore something different from the law of nature, which was held to reflect his ultimate being as decreed by God. According to Isidore, the law of nations is not only valid among nearly all peoples of the earth, but it also corresponds to a higher concept, in this case that of *recta ratio*, enlightened reason.

Isidore sees the following as properly covered by the law of nations: captivity, war, the *postliminium*[1], alliances, peace treaties, truces and the inviolability of embassies.

The Spanish Bishop's definition of the law of nations and the law of nature was repeated in a famous compilation of canon law published about 1140 as "Gratian's Decree". Both authors see the law of nations as applying to the whole of mankind: *"Hoc unde jus gentium appellatur, quia es jure omnes fere gentes utuntur"*.

The definition was to be further clarified by St. Thomas Aquinas and by various writers of the late 13th century who took part in a revival of the study of classical Roman law at the Italian universities. St. Thomas linked the law of nations closely with the law of nature, in which, in fact, he saw its ultimate origin, and the leading Italian commentator of the time on Roman law, Bartole, makes no distinction at all between them. The principles of the law of nations, he maintained, hold good among all peoples and throughout the world. Its principles may, indeed, change, in the course of time, but this is "not inevitable" and, in any case, such changes are always a matter of difficulty.

It therefore follows that for St. Thomas and other mediaeval writers, the law of nations is at once something of superhuman origin and yet a part of man-made law. As such, it drew part of its strength from that body of so-called "positive law" passed freely by human legislators, to which Abélard and the French experts on canon law appear first to have drawn attention in the 12th century.

By the time of St. Thomas, and even earlier — the period of the *divisio regnorum* — a distinction had come to be made between the law of nature and the law of nations on the one hand, and civil or national law on the other, but some centuries had to go by before the law of nations, or international law, achieved its independent status.

Following the precedent of the Roman emperors of antiquity, mediaeval lawyers began to describe the Emperors of the West as law-givers not for the Occident alone, but for the *Universus*

---

[1] Repatriation of prisoners and their re-integration as citizens.

orbis. This was in accordance with the view that the *consuetudo communis*, Roman custom, applied throughout the known world. The claim by the Holy Roman Emperors to be the successors of the Christian emperors of Rome rested legally on the notion of the *translatio*, and the acceptance of Roman law as the law of the Holy Roman Empire had the effect of supporting this claim. Contemporary practices in the field of international relations and especially the frequent mediaeval recourse to arbitration are characteristic of the trend. King Robert of Sicily invoked the pandects and the codex no less than twenty times in his instructions to the legates whom he sent to the Pope in 1319.

In practice, however, from the 12th century onwards, the Imperial power was no longer very effective as a universal lawgiver. The birth of nation-States was at hand and numerous regions of Europe had become or were becoming independent, in fact and in law. Various legal grounds were advanced by rulers to justify their claim to exemption from the Emperor's authority, such as prescription, special privileges granted by the Emperor, ancient custom and even the assumption of irregular titles. The consequence was an ever more widespread non-recognition of the Emperor as a superior authority. Independence for the Kings of France and of England meant that the law of nations was gaining ground, at the expense of centralised law.

The process was to give rise to Bartole's celebrated statement on the break-up of the Holy Roman Empire: "States do not recognize a higher authority than their own": *Civitates non recognoscunt superiorem;* and to Balde's observation: "The King, in his kingdom, is Emperor of that kingdom": *Rex in regno suo est imperator regni*. Politics and law were evolving together in accordance with the needs of the international community.

Jurists of the later Middle Ages make a clear distinction between civil law on the one hand and the law of nature and the law of nations on the other, allotting to each their respective domains. A dignitary of the Church in Styria, Abbot Engelbert Admont, who lived under the Emperor Henry VII at the beginning of the 14th century, said that the King should rule in his kingdom according to a civil law, based on the language, ways and customs of his people. In addition to this, however, there existed a law of nature which was common to all peoples, and also certain principles of the law of nations which all should apply both in their domestic affairs and in their relations with other peoples, whether Christian or pagan. The fact that pagan peoples might live outside the Holy Roman Empire did not prevent their being subject to this law of nature. Here we have a first step towards the concept later expressed by Grotius and Pufendorf that the law of nature and the law of nations do not apply only to Christendom.

As the Holy Roman Empire slowly, but steadily, declined, the formation of national entities gave rise to a new situation. To provide for the relations between this new international community, consisting of nation-States which no longer admitted any common authority higher than their own, a new legal system had to be worked out. The law of nations offered a solution. The new States were taking shape along lines which go back to Aristotle's concept of the *civitas perfecta*. This Aristotelian concept of the State was founded on civil law and the law of nature, so that the law of nations emerged as a governing principle of something quite different, the juridical relations between States. It was Otto von Gierke, the great German legal historian, who first showed how the concept of the law of nations as a part of civil law thus faded out, to be applied henceforth more and more exclusively to strictly international relations.

When the founders of this newly-conceived law of nations wrote their first studies on the subject at the end of the 15th century, the mediaeval concept of an all-powerful Empire considered as the heir of ancient Rome no longer held sway. Vittoria put forward the new concept of the community of nations, the *societas gentium*, obeying one and the same law, namely the *jus gentium*, which was still equated by them with the law of nature or held to derive from it. According to this view, the *societas gentium* was merely an expression of the fundamental unity of the human race and it had nothing to do with an international order or legal system created by the human mind.

Legal theory was dominated by this concept at least until 1612, when the Jesuit Father Suarez, in his *Tractatus de legibus ac Deo legislatore* described the law of nations as being to some extent independent of the law of nature. To admit the law of nations to a fully autonomous status was the great contribution made by Grotius to legal thinking. Being less bound than Suarez to the Thomist doctrine, Grotius, in section 42 of the preliminary discourse to his famous work on the law of war and peace, emphasized that a fundamental distinction exists between the law of nature and the law of nations. "I have been very careful", he wrote, "never to confuse the law of nature and the law of nations".

Grotius, however, approached the problem along pragmatic lines and he offered no clear criterion to distinguish between the two concepts which he was instrumental in separating. His method was to illustrate his thesis by examples, pointing out that the law of nations, unlike the law of nature, rests not on a logical inference from the nature of human beings, but on choice and consent.

The law of nature, said Grotius, offers us all certain principles by which we know whether an act is morally good or bad. The law of nations "derives its authority from the combined will of all the peoples, or at least of many. It often happens that a principle of the law of nations which is accepted in one part of the world does not hold good in another". Grotius did not limit the law of nations to Christian States; like his predecessors he thought that Nature had implanted a kind of kinship in the members of the human race as a whole. A law which was valid only in one country and did not express the accepted views of a number of States, belonged for Grotius to national law and not to the law of nations.

Although its was Grotius who finally established the distinction between the law of nations and the law of nature, he is still not completely clear as to which rules of conduct belong to the domain of each.

The problems raised by this dual concept were solved only after his time and particularly in the 18th century, in part by the German writer Christian Wolff and in part by the Swiss Emer de Vattel, who clarified Wolff's abstract thinking and made it accessible to a larger public. The essential step was taken when Wolff and Vattel claimed precedence for the law of nations over the law of nature, which they reduced to a moral imperative falling outside the legal category.

The new concept was most clearly expressed by Vattel in an essay contest organized by the Academy of Dijon in 1742. The problem to be discussed was whether the law of nature could enable human society to attain perfection without the help of political laws. Vattel affirmed categorically that, in the then state of mankind, the law of nature could not bring the human race to perfection without the help of political laws, in other words of the law of nations. The ignorance and moral frailty of man, he claimed, would prevent his even arriving at the knowledge of the law of nature unless the authorities codified and enforced it through legislation. Wolff and Vattel thus restricted the law of nature to its moral influence on the conscience of man and they robbed it of that precedence over the law of nations which it had enjoyed in legal thinking since the remote period of the Church Fathers.

The last step of all was to be complete abandonment of the concept of a law of nature as such. This we owe to the legal historians of the 19th century. It was they who prepared the way for our contemporary theory of positive law, by their teaching that a legal system is valid only in so far as it is effective. By the same token, we believe that the international legal system is valid only if international law conforms to the actual practice of States and other organizations which enjoy juridical personality.

We have seen how the tripartite classsification of the Church Fathers — law of nature, law of nations, civil law — was succeeded by other concepts and principles with the rise of independent kingdoms in the later Middle Ages. Contemporary thinking on international law allows for only one category of rules — those which in practice govern the behaviour of States in their mutual relations.

International Law in a Changing World
by Professor Radhabinod Pal (India)

Radhabinod Pal: b. 1886. Former Chairman, International Law Commission; 1959: National Professor of Jurisprudence, Government of India; 1946-1948: Judge, International Military Tribunal for the Far East; 1944-1946: Vice-Chancellor, University of Calcutta; 1937: Joint President, International Academy of Comparative Law; 1925, 1930, 1938: Tagore Professor of Law, University of Calcutta.

"Man's hope for world peace does not rest in opposing armed camps, but in an idea", said President Eisenhower. "That idea is the concept of the rule of law as the means for settling disputes among sovereign States. The idea is a simple one. But the acceptance of this course of action by the community of nations is a goal which has eluded man throughout his history."

It is heartening to see that the General Assembly of the United Nations has already directed its attention to the subject we are considering. At its XVth Session, on 12 December 1960, it adopted a resolution on future work in the codification and progressive development of international law, whereby it decided to place the question on the agenda of its XVIth session and also invited Member States to submit their views.

The discussion in the Sixth Committee on this occasion threw a good deal of light on the subject and on the new trends in international relations which make a fresh consideration of it desirable.

In the opinion of some representatives, the activities of the UN in the field of international law have failed to keep pace with the needs of a swiftly moving world. It was pointed out that new elements have been introduced into international law by the granting of independence to many formerly dependent nations, by the economic development of the underdeveloped areas, by swift scientific and technological progress and by the increasing role of international organizations.

Nor should it be forgotten that the world legal community has expanded. The Great Powers are no longer alone responsible for the creation of international law. It is essential that all States, whatever their social and political systems, their geographical location or level of development, should be given a chance to participate in the creation of international law adapted to the world of today. The United Nations in general, and the International Law Commission in particular, it was said, should now play a more creative role. They should foster the growth of new trends which conform to the spirit of the Charter and which encourage co-existence and co-operation. Various speakers pointed out that political, economic and social changes since the Second World War could not fail to have a tremendous impact on contemporary international law. In the first place, the geography of international law has radically changed since its creation was no longer the prerogative of the West. In the second place, international law could no longer serve, as in the past, a relatively homogeneous community, and new problems were arising in connexion with relations between States that had differing political, economic and social systems.

How far ought the forty or so "young" or relatively "young" States to be bound by an international law which they did not help to create and which often runs counter to their interests? It has been suggested that, when a State joins the international community, it thereby automatically undertakes to conform to is rules and institutions. In practice, however, the problem is much more complex and, if numerous rules of international law do not have the active support of a large sector of the international community, the entire machinery for the peaceful settlement of disputes may be in danger.

We are confronted with an unprecedented challenge for justice in international life. After the First World War, which was a "war to end war", we heard many optimistic assurances. In the event, these sadly failed to materialize. World leaders took their post-war problems to be merely their old problems on a broader scale. Failing to grasp that they were new and required new attitudes, these leaders remained faithful to the accepted system of international law which through the centuries had hardened into an elaborate complex of institutions and legal doctrines.

Up to about 1875, the industrial revolution and the emergence of nationalism in the West had been working together to build up the notion of "Great Powers". There was an almost universal fixation of man's social emotions upon national groups. The deep human impulse to feel life as a whole attached itself to particular nations, rather than to the larger society of which those nations were members. This development created a power economy that transformed the face of the earth and brought Asia and Africa under the Western yoke.

After 1875, industrialism and nationalism tended to work in opposite directions. Industrialism began to feel its way towards a worldwide range, by increasing the scale of its operations beyond the compass of the greatest of the Great Powers. Nationalism spread downwards from the leading countries to implant a separate consciousness even in peoples of so small a calibre that they were incapable of forming completely independent States.

As the clash of aspirations increased, world peace came more and more to depend on an uneasy equilibrium of forces. Economic power, already highly concentrated within the nations, developed into international cartels and worldwide monopolies, which bred new international disputes. These disputes, in their own twisted way, were an expression of the new need to enlarge the economic units of the world. The war really established that the world itself was the minimum unit of necessary change.

These facts were not clear to the leaders. The First World War itself, strangely enough, added to the false confidence of mankind. Its remarkable history seemed to confirm the self-regenerating virtues of an economic system which had enabled large societies to feed and clothe themselves, even in the anarchy of universal war. Politicians believed that such an economic system could be trusted to solve its own problems. And so they discussed indemnities and colonies, putting national desires first and world needs second. The abandonment of the spirit of the League Covenant finally drove the world towards the catastrophe of a second war. It should be evident by now that we are still caught in a tangle of causes and circumstances which is sweeping us towards something that nobody wants. The world is being driven deeper into an epoch of permanent war.

In Asia live a billion people, all but a tiny fraction of whom are still condemned to live in a degrading poverty and primitive backwardness on a continent rich in land and wealth, in all human and material resources. This condition started centuries ago when the Western Powers reached out aggressively for the wealth of the East. The period after the war was marked by great political upheavals in various parts of the world. In Asia the end of the war touched off impulses of a gigantic force. Huge masses of poverty-ridden, dominated people entered the political arena in search of independence: a billion people had to keep on struggling to win even a semblance of political freedom; a billion had to thrash around in search of a way out. International society, however, could offer no manner of renewal or adjustment except through death and destruction. Western imperialism, though hopelessly incapable of fostering growth, was strong enough to drive progressive Asiatic nationalism back into the suffocating soil of social and economic backwardness. It was also able to prostitute various colonial and semi-colonial ruling classes to its own purposes.

Thus when the world was brought to the Second World War in the course of a few years many felt that the old foundation of the international order itself had been damaged beyond, perhaps, the possibility of repair. Any reshaping of the order of international relations might involve the need to construct a new base altogether.

Amid immense slaughter and suffering, the issue of world power came out hanging in the balance between the two giants, Russia and the United States, who succeeded in surviving the war with strength enough to become rivals for the domination of the world in one form or another. What thus survived the war was national and economic power in its most highly concentrated form, and the world had to devise a political machine only for securing the maximum possible amount of co-operation between these two powers.

The above account may appear disheartening in its tendency to emphasize human selfishness. We know that international law depends for its effectiveness almost entirely on the element of moral obligation to others. Goodwill is essential to its success and we seem to have noted an absence of goodwill on the part of national leaders. The fact is, however, that those leaders are just as good or as bad, just as wise or as stupid, as rulers in general always have been. If statesmen whose sense of moral obligation is otherwise keen disregard the claims of international law, it is perhaps because they sense that that law has drifted away from the realities of world politics.

It may be appropriate here to draw attention to one more aspect of modern progress which affects man's capacity to judge broad issues. This is the tendency to overspecialization, by which scholars and other intellectual leaders add to knowledge within ever narrower limitations of subject matter. This modern tendency produces "minds in a groove" without the necessary broad grasp of the forces which are shaping the world we live in. The tendency is particularly dangerous in democratic societies, for the leading intellects are not trained to appreciate more than one set of circumstances. Ideologies tend to taint our knowledge, making our apprehension of truth something more like knowledge of "our truth", which is less than knowledge of "the truth". This is why everyone declares his love for peace, when he means his own particular peace on his own terms. The simple distinction so often made between "truth" and "error" leads to the terrible illusion that "our truth" must use coercion as well as persuasion to destroy opposing beliefs. This distinction ignores the ambiguous character of historical knowledge, and ignores both the possibility of residual error in the purest truth and the saving truth even in obvious error.

The end of the First World War can be taken as the starting-point of a new phase of the international order. It marks the pioneering enterprise of substituting the human device of some sort of constitutional control for the blind play of physical force in the conduct of international relations. It has already been amply indicated how this First World War itself emerged with all its accumulated forces out of a long series of events following in the track of what is characterized as the industrial revolution.

In this phase of the industrial revolution, however, the military factor exercised no material effect. Its main instrument was the steam engine, introduced to save human labour in industry and thus coming to occupy a central position in the industrial economy. This is a point of fundamental importance. Military factors had played no role in bringing about the industrial revolution nor did they impel it forward, or accelerate its technical processes. Now, for the first time in history, the main source of technical revolutions has moved to the military sphere. Military leaders have joined hands with the scientists and are introducing the military revolution as a dynamic factor in development as a whole.

The difference, indeed, is a fundamental one. So much so that we shall have to exert all our mental powers in order to realize its full implications and to avoid the fatal mistake of regarding it in the false light of any superficial analogies suggested by the past.

For nearly twenty-five centuries, the atom has intrigued the world's greatest philosphers and scientists. Many have sensed that within the atom a powerful force is held captive, and have searched for ways to free this energy, so that it could be harnessed to serve useful purposes for mankind. The answer was found, unfortunately, at a time when the released force could be thought of only as a terrible destructive agent. What the released force was made to do can hardly be called an "accomplishment".

No doubt, gain in material power affords an opportunity for social betterment. If mankind can rise to the occasion, there may lie in front of us a golden age. Material power in itself, however, is ethically neutral. It can equally well work in the wrong direction. It may be that humanity will very soon find out that the atom has been smashed too soon.

We all know something of the importance of nuclear power

and its significance in the economic world to-day. We are assured that it can be a great force for the benefit of mankind. At the same time, so novel a power as this undoubtedly raises great technological problems and certainly it will raise legal problems of unforeseen magnitude, both national and international.

Indeed, the peaceful uses of atomic energy are likely to open up a huge and far-reaching field of industrial activity, not only through the atom itself but through the whole sub-atomic field and a variety of types of radiated energy. There will be many things too dangerous to keep, yet too valuable to throw away.

We must remember that in the practical application of the knowledge won in the sphere of atomic physics the military sphere was, and still is, ahead of the economic and industrial spheres. I believe that until the discovery of the atom, and then of the hydrogen bomb, the military mind has never been in the van of human thinking. Never did a situation arise in which scientific and technical developments in the military sphere were ahead of, and therefore in a position to react on, the ordinary economic-industrial sphere.

The military-atomic revolution to-day is the determining factor in industrial and economic development, but the two are not proceeding at anything like the same pace. The scientists and technicians working in the service of the military revolution have enormous funds at their disposal, without having to work under the controlling discipline of profit considerations. The result has been to drive the process of development in this field forward in a cataclysmic rush. The pace of industrial development in this same period has not been even remotely analogous. Atomic energy for peaceful purposes is moving only very slowly into production.

It is necessary only to mention such now familiar expressions as intermediate-range ballistic missiles, intercontinental ballistic missiles, even interplanetary ballistic missiles, to suggest why everyone of us feels tense, uncertain, adrift. To add to this almost all the relevant conditions surrounding the international legal order are in a phase of terrifying transformation. None of the key elements in that order has remained untouched by the changes.

The structure of the State system, the purposes that inspire State policies and the means available to States for carrying out those policies, are all changing under our eyes.

At the same time, we have seen the international community itself broadened to include Asian and African nations. Those who say that this broadening has weakened the moral basis of the international legal system forget that that moral basis was fatally weakened long before the geographical expansion of the international community occurred. Society before the industrial era, based as it was on agriculture and handicrafts, depended on personal ties and was governed by a personal ethic. Industrialism shattered both the ties and the ethic. A new code arose to deal with more remote, statistical units of business and the gap between personal morality and economic practice widened in an alarming way. Making the most of one's opportunities constituted an efficient morality for the industrialists of the period.

International law as seen in the 19th century was therefore largely a limitation placed on political authority in the interests of individual freedom of initiative. The first fundamental change in this respect occurred during World War I when industry and trade were regulated for political ends. The laws of supply and demand were discarded and political expediency determined production and consumption, wages and prices. A necessary consequence of this extension of State interest was that the State assumed responsibility for the individual worker and his security. The State claimed unlimited control over the citizen, but it also began to assume responsibility for his material existence. Nationalism and imperialism considered the State as merely an instrument in the service of enterprising individuals, but in our time we have seen individual self-determination abdicate in favour of the all-embracing power of the State.

From the point of view of international conflicts, this has meant that, while private economic interests were often at the root of earlier disputes, such conflicts now arise from the tendency we have noted to secure freedom of action for governments. International law must obviously be concerned with this extended activity of the State. Formerly, the international legal order was based on the dualism of private life and public authority, but there has been a fundamental change in this respect almost everywhere in the world. Today, no branch of international law can be allowed to remain the prisoner of concepts evolved under different circumstances and for different purposes.

There is nothing new in the existence of different social organisms in the world at the same time. The fundamental difference is that now they continually react and interact on one another. This, indeed, is perhaps the most typical characteristic and need of our age. Human wisdom must be devoted to building up a new world structure which will provide for the co-ordination of different social systems in one international order. Any separation of legal values from existing realities is likely to provoke a crisis in the international community. Law has to operate not merely as an ideal which relies on the governments' sense of moral obligation, but on the necessary functional order in the structure of political relationships. Law must become more political, if politics is to become more law-abiding.

I have not concealed a certain sense of frustration in regard to past efforts. Every government, every people, every one of us, shares a responsibility for the future and for realizing the full meaning of the changes amidst which we live. Mistakes now may easily prove irremediable. We must not be complacent or believe so readily in the inevitability of success.

The Expanding Frontiers of Public International Law
by Dr. T. O. Elias

T. O. Elias: Attorney-General of the Federation of Nigeria and Minister of Justice; 1956: Visiting Professor in Political Science, Delhi University; former Research Fellow, University of Oxford Institute of Commonwealth Studies and Nuffield College; Research Fellow in Law, University of Manchester; Research Fellow, UNESCO; author of several volumes on African Law and Government.

Public international law today is undergoing rapid changes, both in its rules of substantive law and in the extent of its jurisdiction. On the substantive law side, one may wish to re-state the provisions of Article 38 of the Statute of the International Court of Justice at The Hague, which prescribes that the Court shall have regard to the following four sources of international law: —

1. (a) International conventions, whether general or particular, establishing rules expressly recognised by the contesting parties;
   (b) International custom, as evidence of a general practice accepted as law;
   (c) The general principles of law recognized by civilised nations;
   (d) Subject to the provisions of Article 59, judicial decisions and the teachings of the most highly qualified publicists of the various nations, as subsidiary means for the determination of rules of law.
2. This provision shall not prejudice the power of the Court to decide a case *ex sequo et bono,* if the parties agree thereto.

It will be noticed at once that the inclusion in 1 (a) of international treaties, agreements and conventions is noteworthy as it can easily be shown that, in this particular field, the growth of international law has been most remarkable. One recalls, for example, The Hague Conventions of 1907, the League Covenant, the Statute of the Permanent Court of International Justice, the Briand-Kellogg Pact of 1928, the United Nations Charter, the Statute of the International Court of Justice, the various conventions and studies established by the United Nations Economic and Social Council, and such specialised agencies of the United Nations as the Food and Agriculture Organisation, and the World Health Organisation, as well as the substantial body of conventions such as those of the European Human Rights Commission of 1948. All these have done a great deal to deepen our knowledge of the detailed rules of international law in their special fields, and also to remove the uncertainties and vagueness that previously characterised international law.

It is gradually becoming less and less fashionable for critics of public international law to sneer at it by pointing to the fact that it lacks supranational authority and political sovereignty, both of which are regarded as indispensable to a body of law properly so-called. While it is true that international law still lacks the political concept of sovereignty so long as the various States are not prepared to submit to a sovereign body under a world government, it is nevertheless the case that by the increasing acceptance of the rule of law in international relations and by the progressive filling up of gaps in the body of the rules of international law, the world is moving in the direction of an ultimate recognition of supremacy of the rule of law in the international society. It is significant that the United Nations Organisation attached the greatest importance to this aspect of the matter by the establishment of the International Law Commisssion charged with the specific responsibility for studying the weak and ill-defined areas of public international law and making available for the General Assembly detailed draft rules and conventions thereon, with a view to the progressive development of international law. It would be unnecessary to attempt to demonstrate within the compass of this short essay the value and importance of the contribution to our knowledge of international law which the International Law Commission of the United Nations has made in the past decade.

Even in the sphere of customary international law, that is, the rules and principles of international behaviour universally accepted as law, there has been a healthy widening of the international horizon. It will be recalled that throughout the 18th and 19th centuries, international society led by the Great Powers assumed that public international law did not really extend to nations that could not be described as "civilised". This exclusive character of public international law resulted in a country like China, with probably a much longer historical tradition of culture and enlightenment than many of the States of Western Europe at that time, being excluded from the purview of international law.

It was not until the conference on the Treaty of Versailles in 1919 that the first effort was made to allow certain dependent countries like India to be represented along with the then sovereign States. There has, of course, been a more definitive attitude on the part of both the old League of Nations and the United Nations towards the Dominions of the British Commonwealth, all of which have since taken their due places as full and sovereign members of both organisations. One observation that may be made in this respect is the difference between the number of States that formerly made up the membership of the League of Nations and the number of those that became sovereign Members of the United Nations established in 1945; a further testimony to the great change that has taken place in the United Nations itself may be seen in the fact that, whereas there were only some fifty State Members in 1945, there are today over one hundred.

A corollary of this widening of the frontiers of public international law is the emergence on the world scene since 1947 of the new nations of Asia and Africa. The Bandung Conference of Afro-Asian countries has produced what is now commonly referred to as the Afro-Asian bloc at the United Nations Headquarters in New York. This group of former dependencies of the Great Powers has lost no time in asserting its rights to increased participation in the work of the UN and its various organs. This has led to a great deal of re-thinking on the part of the other States Members who have shown a remarkable degree of readiness to concede worthwhile claims of this kind. There can be little doubt that this reasonable attitude accounts for the fact that the present Secretary-General of the United Nations is U Thant, a Burmese, and that the President of the Sixteenth Session of the General Assembly was Mongi Slim, a Tunisian, and this trend is observable in most of the other organs of the United Nations where Asia and Africa are now represented.

We may now turn to another aspect of the transformation which the emergence of States formerly regarded as outside the pale of public international law is, whether consciously or unconsciously, helping to bring about. It will be sufficient to mention three of these, with particular reference to Africa. In the first place, all the African States Members of the United Nations are determined to form themselves into a distinct African group with the sole purpose of pressing their special claims upon the attention of the world organisation. Attention may be drawn to certain resolutions adopted at the Conference of Heads of African and Malagasy States held in Lagos, Nigeria, from 25th to 30th January, 1962 to the effect that: —

"(a) the African and Malagasy Members of the United Nations Organisation should constitute themselves into a definite group in dealing with all the problems, particularly those that are peculiar to Africa and Madagascar, that may henceforth come before the United Nations;

(b) this group should strive continuously to obtain a revision of the Charter in order to have a fair and equitable representation of African and Malagasy States on the Security Council, Economic and Social Council, the Secretariat and other organs of the United Nations."

The Conference drew attention to Article 23(1) of the United Nations Charter which refers to "equitable geographical distribution" of seats on the Security Council, pointing out that while Europe, Latin America and Asia are adequately and substantially represented thereon, Africa does not at present enjoy this particular status. Delegate after delegate rose to stress that when the Charter of the United Nations was originally drawn up, the countries of Asia and Africa were not taken into serious consideration as likely Members of the United Nations, at least on the scale that these countries have since become Members. The Conference therefore felt that the time has come for a wholesale review of the Charter itself so as to ensure that the organisation reflects more faithfully the contemporary patterns of an international society that now embraces nearly two-thirds of the world population that was previously excluded from the purview of international law. It must be recognised, however, that the Conference attached the greatest importance to the continued membership in the United Nations of African and Malagasy States; indeed, Article 32 of the proposed Charter of Inter-African and Malagasy States Organisation provides as follows: —

"The High Contracting Parties agree that nothing herein shall be understood or interpreted as impairing the rights and obligations of member States of the Inter-African and Malagasy Organisation under the Charter of the United Nations Organisation."

On the question of the registration and interpretation of this Lagos Charter, after due ratification by the States parties to it, Article 37 further provides as follows: —

"The High Contracting Parties agree that the present Charter shall after due ratification be registered with the Secretariat of the United Nations through the Government of ....
in conformity with Article 103, of the Charter of the United Nations."

It is therefore clear that the proposed organisation for Africa has not been conceived of as a rival organisation to the UN, or even as a substitute for it. It is no more than an enlarged form of the "regional arrangements" and groupings which Article 52 of the United Nations Charter encourages or permits so long as the purpose is the fostering of international peace and security.

Another development in international law which African States will foster is in respect of a re-appraisal of the legal status of certain treaties entered into by the Colonial Powers in Africa with other sovereign States before the grant of political independence to their former dependent territories. It is the view of most of the African States today that the customary rules and principles governing State succession could not properly be applied in their entirety to them so as to make them liable to assume obligations imposed under such treaties. It is felt that, at independence, the former Colonial Powers usually entered into a form of agreement whereby the African country about to be granted independence would assume responsibility for all the rights and obligations arising under all existing treaties between the Metropolitan Power and other sovereign States, and that the newly independent States should be entitled to review such treaties with a view to modifying or replacing these wherever this course should prove to be in their best interests. In short, they claim that this is a case to which the defence of *clausula rebus sic stantibus* ought eminently to apply. The importance of the legal issue raised in this connection can be gauged when it is realised that a new body, the "Committee on succession of new States to the treaties and other obligations of their predecessors" set up by the International Law Asssociation of Great Britain, is already at work endeavouring to produce a body of new and acceptable principles of State succession.

Yet another interesting contribution that Africa may make to the development of public international law lies in the military and economic spheres. On the military side, the new sovereign nations of Africa are jealous of their independence, and many of them do not appreciate the need for military alliances like NATO, or the Warsaw Pact, or even such recent agreements for mutual defence assistance as were entered into between Britain and certain of her former dependencies and between France and her own. These countries are prepared to jettison such means of buttressing the territorial integrity of their countries in favour of maintaining their rugged independence in an uncertain world situation. Nevertheless, they do not necessarily eschew any informal arrangements either with their former Metropolitan Powers or with other Great Powers if, as the saying goes, "there are no strings attached." Here, indeed, is some recognition on the part of these States that while they do require technical and organisational assistance from the more developed nations, yet they shrink from any arrangement that could sometimes make this possible. This is a challenge to modern international law which could make a contribution to the cause of world peace by devising machinery for the attainment of these purposes.

Everyone will probably agree that a matter of considerable significance in modern international law is the provision in Article 2(7) of the United Nations Charter which precludes the possibility of any form of intervention in what is regarded as "within the domestic jurisdiction" of a State Member of the Organisation. Thus has South Africa successfully refused to allow the United Nations to investigate allegations of oppression and racial discrimination against Africans in that territory; France has done the same thing in respect of Algeria up to the time of the recent truce; Portugal, in respect of Angola, Fernando Po and Mozambique; but, recently, while Great Britain upheld the sanctity of this clause of the United Nations Charter, she has graciously agreed to allow the affairs of Southern Rhodesia, a self-governing colony, to be investigated by the special committee recently set up by the United Nations Organisation. It seems very urgent and necesssssary that Article 2(7) of the United Nations Charter should be reviewed with a view to effecting suitable modifications which would permit of intervention by the United Nations on humanitarian grounds. That such an exercise would require the utmost care and circumspection to avoid unwarranted infringement of sovereignty of a State Member is undeniable; otherwise, the proclamation in the United Nations Charter that the Organisation is based upon the political sovereignty and territorial integrity of all its Members could be in jeopardy. Africa has now the largest number of dependent territories of Metroppolitan Powers and, if threats to world peace are to be avoided in the near future, public international law has a special responsibility to ensure that causes of friction are reduced to a minimum.

Public international law is therefore at its most dynamic and exciting stage of development, embracing as it does new nations of different colours, creeds and social and economic circumstances, who together make up modern international society. The challenge of the times requires it to show itself capable of adaptation and expansion in order to enable it to fulfill its destiny, which is, in a sense, to foster the conversion of the present international society into a truly international community, based upon respect for human dignity and the supremacy of the rule of law.

Law and Outer Space
by Sir Leslie Munro (New Zealand)

Sir Leslie Munro: b.1901. 1957: President, 12th Session, United Nations General Assembly; 1952: New Zealand Ambassador to United States and Permanent Representative to United Nations; served as President, United Nations Security Council and Trusteeship Council, and Chairman, First (Political) Committee, General Assembly; 1942-1951: Editor, New Zealand Herald; *former lecturer in Roman law and constitutional law and history, Auckland University College, New Zealand; Secretary-General, International Commission of Jurists.*

One of the reasons for my special interest in this subject is that I happened to be President of the General Assembly of the United Nations when the first sputnik was launched. If there are any people who still think the subject of law and outer space to be remote or unrealistic, I am afraid that the march of events will disillusion them. I have even heard of a distinguished statesman saying that we had enough to do on earth without worrying about the law of outer space.

Against that narrow point of view, I would suggest that man's entry into space and the propulsion of satellites round the earth must herald a new vision of the universe. I would also suggest that, for a comparable impact upon the human mind, you would have to go back to the Renaissance and the discovery of America. And yet, to call those events of the fifteenth and sixteenth centuries comparable to our ventures would be to minimise the vastness of our hopes and fears in the nuclear age.

What is the situation today? A Russian has orbited the earth in a space vehicle. An American has been propelled some eighty miles above the earth and has come down safely on the Atlantic Ocean. These are only preliminary achievements in the exploration of space. In the book entitled "Controls for Outer Space" the distinguished lawyers Jessup and Tauberfield state that, if the necessary funds are forthcoming, man may reach the moon as early as 1963 and might even send an 8-man rocket to Mars by 1970. Soviet scientists have talked of putting men on the moon or even on the planets by 1965. Jessup and Tauberfield, basing their estimate on speeds obtainable in 1959, say that a journey from the earth to Mercury would take 110 days. However, it is well to remember that new developments are continually revolutionizing our concepts of speed and travel.

Not only in regard to such aspects of space are we on the threshold of a new era in human thinking. We have entered a new age in the realm of navigation, communications, weather forecasts and even control of weather in such a way as to affect the capacity of nations to resist aggression, examination and mapping of the earth and moon, knowledge of what is happening in every part of the world, including nuclear explosions. It is a truism that all these developments and possibilities have political and military implications.

It was long said that the race which was master of the mountains of Bohemia was the master of Europe. Now, we hear it said that the power which can land on and control the moon will be master of the earth.

I agree with Jessup and Tauberfield that the military implications of the new mastery of space can be ignored only as a result of wilful blindness or political convenience. I am one of a number of people who have urged that an international agency under the United Nations be established to control the use of outer space for peaceful purposes. Speaking to the Royal Military College at Kingston, Ontario, on 15 May 1959, the Prime Minister of Canada, Mr. Diefenbaker said: "The promotion and establishment of the rule of law is now necessary and outer space should belong to the world as a whole. Jurisdiction should be vested in the United Nations to ensure that it will be used for scientific and peaceful purposes only. All nations, great and small, should have equal territorial rights and the launching of all space missiles should be preceded by notification that benefits accruing will therefore be available to all mankind."

You will note his emphasis on prior notification of all space missiles, and it is certainly true that the United States, when launching its first astronaut into space gave clear notice of what it was intending. Since we learnt of the launching of the first sputnik, I have urged that the United Nations is the proper forum for discussion of the problems resulting from man's penetration of the universe. Perhaps, as the representative of a small nation, I am not without bias in this matter. In the Assembly, the small nations of the world can make their voice heard and they can be represented on appropriate committees. Apart from this aspect of the question, it seems to me that there is an identity between the purpose of the United Nations and the principles which must govern any international consideration of problems relating to outer space. The peaceful use of space devices will surely involve some programme of international control. Moreover, the benefits derived from such devices must be shared by all nations. This tendency has been accentuated in another very new field, that of atomic energy, through the creation of the International Atomic Energy Agency. Other evidence of the same trend could be found in the International Geophysical Year and in the vast area of Antarctica, where international co-operation between the powers, including the Soviet Union, has been singularly fruitful.

In this connexion, I would recall to you the existence of the International Civil Aviation Organization (ICAO). This organization might undertake new responsibilities beyond air space, if the Soviet Union were willing to participate and to ratify a new treaty.

In all such international organizations, a question arises concerning national sovereignty. When we come to consider outer space we shall find that national sovereignty there is connected with the history of claims to jurisdiction by States over the air space above them. By 1919, when aviation was already playing an important part in our world, it was generally recognized that each State has full and absolute sovereignty over the air above its territories and territorial waters, a sovereignty that carries with it the right to exclude foreign aircraft. Both the United States and the Soviet Union have firmly enunciated this principle. In fact, the first article of the 1944 Chicago Convention states that: "The contracting States recognize that every State has complete and exclusive authority over the air space above its territory." Some people have maintained that you would be entitled to bring an action for trespass against an aircraft flying above your land by appealing to the Roman maxim that ownership involves everything above and below the surface of your land. I believe there was such a claim by a citizen of the United States, but it was not admitted. Nevertheless, States have held to their assertion of sovereignty over the air space above them.

The difficulty begins when you try to define air space. It seems clear that national sovereignty does not extend to outer space, but there is considerable controversy as to where air space ends and outer space begins.

An American expert, Col. Martin Menter of the United States Air Force has published a paper entitled "Astronautical Law". According to this expert as men leave the earth for outer space they will pass successively through five layers of atmosphere, a number which other authorities sometimes reduce to four. Col. Menter's picture is as follows:

(a) The troposphere extends upwards from the earth to about ten miles. However, only about 20 per cent of the troposphere contains oxygen and supplementary oxygen is necessary to maintain life above 15,000 feet.

(b) Next comes the stratosphere extending to about 16 miles. At about half way through the stratosphere, blood would boil, while the outside temperature would be 70° below zero Fahrenheit.

(c) Beyond the stratosphere, the mesophere extends to about 50 miles.

(d) The thermisphere reaches beyond the stratosphere for 200 to 300 miles. It is also known as the ionosphere, due to its intense electrical activity.

(e) The exosphere extends to perhaps a thousand miles beyond the earth and there bends into outer space, with which we are mainly concerned. Jessup and Tauberfield, in the book I have referred to, regard the exosphere as already a part of interplanetary space.

In a book of mine entitled "United Nations — Hope for a Divided World" I have pointed out that no government has yet questioned the right of either the United States or the Soviet Union to send satellites through outer space, wherever may be the precise point at which outer space is considered to begin. No government has claimed that its sovereignty is infringed when a missile hurtles above its territory through outer space.

This leaves some interesting questions unanswered. For example, when flying at its highest altitude, did the U-2 violate Soviet air space if no Soviet aircraft or missile was capable of hitting it at that altitude? You will recall that there is controversy as to whether it was hit at that high altitude or whether it had to come down. One eminent lawyer has maintained that, if the U-2 was forced to descend through some mechanical fault and was then hit by a Soviet projectile, the American plane was within the area of Soviet sovereignty. If it was flying above the area where it could be hit, he contended that there was some question as to whether it was infringing Soviet sovereignty.

Some experts are opposed to a distinction being made between air space and outer space. From a practical, military point of view, they maintain that air space and outer space merge into one, forming a continuous and indivisible field of operations.

Here we are touching upon very practical considerations indeed, concerned not only with the formulation of law, such as you and I might wish to see, but with power and the exercise of it.

My own view is that, for the purpose of international law, embryonic as it may be in this field, there is nevertheless a difference between air space and outer space. On the other hand, at this stage of our knowledge, it may be unwise to attempt a precise definition of where one ends and the other begins. A pragmatic approach to the subject suggests that our present knowledge is insufficient for us to define the limits of air space or of sovereignty. The establishment of a convention for the control of outer space, and the enunciation of the principles dealing with it, would seem, from this point of view, premature. There are some who think that too precise an agreement now might prove an embarrassment when our knowledge and experience of the possibilities grows.

One of the most fascinating aspects of the problem of outer space is the question of jurisdiction and sovereignty over celestial bodies, the moon and the planets. For anybody to have raised this question ten years ago would have seemed to most people a sign of incipient insanity. Now, however, our romantic moon has actually been hit by a body hurled from the Soviet Union. At the moment when that impact occurred, the moon seemed to come very much closer to us and the nature of its influence on our lives changed profoundly. Maybe, even Mars will be reached in our lifetime. Most of us here are almost certain to see men land on the moon. Will they exercise a right of ownership on behalf of their country? My own view is that, in the present state of international law, the gaining of title by occupation, possession and settlement does not apply to a landing on the moon.

On 19 May 1958, the Secretary-General of the United Nations expressed the hope that, as a result of its deliberations, the General Assembly would find its way to an agreement by which outer space and the celestial bodies would be considered as incapable of being appropriated by any State. In the case of Antarctica, even nations maintaining territorial claims there have agreed not to press them at the present time. Will nations display a similar wisdom over the moon, which surely is not susceptible to discovery, occupation and settlement as we now understand these terms?

When we come to consider the possibility of exercising international jurisdiction over the moon and the planets, the question arises as to the organ by which such jurisdiction could be exercised. One might turn to the United Nations itself or establish a form of trusteeship, with certain designated nations acting on its behalf. However, in the present state of international relations, the familiar problem of the veto would be likely to assert itself. I myself am therefore not too optimistic on this point, although I believe that we should all work patiently and consistently for the Secretary-General's guiding objective that no State should have sovereignty over any celestial body. It will be necessary in any event to approach these subjects with great patience, as we have seen in the long negotiations that have taken place in such related fields as disarmament and the cessation of nuclear tests.

You will recall that in December 1958 a majority of members of the General Assembly voted to establish an *ad hoc* committee, whose task was to report on the peaceful uses of outer space and particularly on the future organizational arrangements which might be made by the United Nations. Unfortunately, three of the States invited to send representatives to serve on the committee did not do so and the remaining members of the committee acted with great caution. They were Argentina, Australia, Belgium, Brazil, Canada, Czechoslovakia, France, Iran, Italy, Japan, Mexico, Poland, Sweden, the United Kingdom, and the United States. Absentees were India, the United Arab Republic and the Soviet Union. The committee refrained from attempting to determine the precise limits between air space and outer space and from recommending international commitments in regard to the contamination of outer space or of the air from outer space. They also avoided recommending rules governing the exploration, settlement and exploitation of celestial bodies and rules for the avoidance of interference among space vehicles.

It was agreed that no existing agency should be asked to undertake overall responsibility for space matters and it was also agreed that not enough was yet known about the possible uses of outer space to make a comprehensive code of laws practical or desirable at the present time. A suggestion was made that a small unit be set up to serve as a focal point for co-operation and to advise the Secretary-General. In the absence of broader international co-operation, it would perhaps have been difficult to recommend any more far-reaching steps than these.

At the present time, realistic thinking compels us to bear in mind that only two countries have hitherto been able to report any really effective achievements in regard to outer space and this fact alone has implied an additional emphasis on the enormous influence and power which those two States exert. Under the competitive conditions which at present obtain and in view of the political and military implications involved, it would be difficult, though perhaps not impossible, to separate the military from the non-military uses of outer space. A decision to internationalize the development of outer space would presuppose a far-reaching agreement on the control of arms and on their development. Once you approach the question of control and inspection of sites from which projectiles are launched through outer space to another area of the globe, you are obviously entering upon a most delicate area of military strategy.

I myself feel very strongly that the longer we postpone attempts at international agreements on the use of outer space, the more difficult the solution of the problem will be. I agree with the Australian representative who told the First Committee of the General Assembly in November 1958: "Experience in Antarctica may suggest how difficult it may become to consider the problems of outer space impartially and on a universal plane, if a decision is left until States have established themselves permanently in the future."

In my view, our goal must be the establishment of an international agency under the aegis of the United Nations or perhaps an agreement similar to that which appears to have been reached in the case of Antarctica. The achievement of such a settlement must depend, for all practical purposes, upon an agreement between the two leading powers in the sphere of outer space development. In a document submitted to the United Nations by the Soviet Union, some form of international control was proposed, though it was attached to conditions regarding the evacuation of overseas bases. As I said in my book, the essential point is that, pending an agreement, the subject of outer space has come within the purview of the United Nations, for it properly belongs with that repository of the hopes and aspirations of mankind. However, it can be solved only if all Members of the world organization, great and small, are ready to rise above national and ideological prejudices.

I am afraid that the omens are not good and it seems likely

that insistence upon the right of veto in an agency dealing with outer space, which is a condition to be expected, does not hold out much hope for a convention in which the will of the majority will prevail.

Nevertheless, in the realm of Antarctica we do seem to have reached some sort of understanding and there has been a great exchange of scientific knowledge gained in that icy area. As against this, the exchange of information regarding the propulsion of vehicles in outer space does not yet appear to have been very encouraging. Maybe in a year or so we shall enter upon a new era, as I profoundly hope, but at the present time I see no reason for any great optimism.

The Development of International Humanitarian Law
by Jean S. Pictet (Switzerland)

Jean S. Pictet: b.1914. 1946: Director, International Committee of the Red Cross, Geneva; 25 years as official of the ICRC; throughout Second World War collaborated closely in all Red Cross activities with President, ICRC, Prof. Max Huber; 1946-1949: responsible for preparatory work and draft texts leading to the Geneva Conventions of 1949 for the protection of war victims.

It has been said that war is the earliest and most important form of organized relations between the peoples and some writers claim that we have a record of only 250 years of general peace in over 3,000 years of written history.

Through the centuries, man has sought to use violence against his fellows in order to give himself a better chance of survival. Being unable to replace war by law, he has nevertheless sought in various ways to limit its horrors and to "humanize" it. A certain chivalry based on mutual advantage led to the acceptance of "rules of the game", which were to be a starting point for a law of war. Thus, in a sense, it was warfare that gave birth to international law, following the efforts of various pioneers to introduce some principles of humanity and mercy even into the midst of violence. The ultimate result of their endeavours will, one hopes, be to efface war and its ravages from the memory of man.

In classical times, the Stoic philosophers were already uttering counsels of moderation such as the saying *hostes dum vulnerati fratres*. They did not, however, extend these charitable precepts to the "barbarians", who were regarded as fit subjects for slavery. Christian teachers introduced the noble concept of disinterested love for one's fellows and included all mankind within their charity. But, in practice, warriors tended to apply such precepts only in wars between fellow Christians, and it has to be admitted that Saladin was the most humane fighter in the Crusades.

During the Middle Ages, a certain mystic value and educational power was attributed to suffering but, at their close, scholastic writers such as Vittoria began to postulate a "law of nature", which they described as of Divine origin. It was urged that, in accordance with that law, war should be conducted in such a way as to avoid useless suffering, but these writers found their efforts largely frustrated by the unfortunate distinction between just and unjust wars. It was long held that those who fought in what was called a just cause could deal with the enemy as they thought fit.

After the Reformation, Grotius and his disciples began to promote the development of international law in the name of reason. What we describe as the scientific spirit was beginning to guide human thinking. One consequence of the new study of the world and of man himself was that human life began to be regarded from the standpoint of human rights. The "Age of Enlightenment" saw the real beginnings of that aspect of modern humanitarianism which is a rational form of charity and of man's demand for justice. It fell to two Swiss citizens, Vattel and Jean-Jacques Rousseau, to give classic expression to the principles of humanitarian law. In his *"Contrat Social"*, Rousseau made the famous statement that war is not a relationship between man and man, but between State and State, a relationship in which individuals are enemies by accident, not as men but as soldiers. Rousseau insisted that, since the object of war was the destruction of the enemy State, soldiers had the right to kill those who defended that State as long as they bore arms. However, once they yielded their arms or surrendered, they became ordinary men again and no one had a right to take their lives. At the time of the French Revolution, these ideas were widely proclaimed, together with the "inalienable right" of the wounded to be cared for and of prisoners of war to be the responsibility of the nation which took them prisoner.

The 18th century saw various agreements between army commanders to deal with wounded and prisoners of war in a humane manner. Such agreements, however, applied only to the circumstances in which they were concluded and the wars of the French Revolution itself and the Empire, by introducing conscription and mass campaigns, were to mark a grim setback for the humanitarians.

Many years had to go by before the young Genevese, Henri Dunant, became by accident a witness at Solférino of the sufferings of the wounded. Forty thousand of these died of infection after being neglected for days, when medical care could have saved a great many of them. Haunted by the ghastly scene, Dunant wrote his pamphlet *"Un Souvenir de Solférino"*. In these prophetic pages he suggested the foundation of the Red Cross and an international agreement to protect military hospitals and personnel.

With the support of some noble-hearted citizens of Geneva, the Red Cross was founded in 1863 and its International Committee soon brought together the diplomats of 16 States, who adopted the "Geneva Convention for the Amelioration of the Condition of the Wounded and Sick in Armed Forces in the Field".

Few realise the capital importance in the development of international law which we can attribute to the ten articles of this Convention. By thus creating an inviolable area, where shot and shell could not penetrate, 16 States agreed, probably for the first time in history, to set limits to their own sovereign power. What had been in practice a sporadic and hesitating custom was given the status of a universal law, valid everywhere and for all time. Henceforth, in this particular sphere, the political and military interests of States were no longer paramount and a breach had been made in the principle of sovereignty itself. Even in the flaming heat of battle, the voice of mercy was to be heard. The wounded soldier was to be cared for, from whichever side his wounds or weapons came.

This treaty has become the cornerstone of all subsequent humanitarian law. By successive stages, its principles, limited at first to wounded soldiers, have been extended to other war victims such as prisoners, survivors of shipwrecks and civilians. All these are now covered by the four Geneva Conventions of 1949, which in our day probably represent three-quarters of the existing international law of war. Other regulations have strengthened the humanitarian tendency inaugurated by the first Geneva Convention. Already in 1863 the United States proclaimed the "Lieber Laws", which were to exert a powerful influence in this field. In 1868 came the monumental work of Bluntschli, *"Codified International Law"*, which included the great principle: "The law of war is intended to civilise just and unjust wars alike." It so happens that the notion of an unjust war has returned in our time, as applied to a war of aggression. Nowadays, however, a distinction is made between the *jus ad bellum*, concerning the recourse to war, and the *jus in bello*, on behaviour in war, which latter applies in all hostilities.

The humanitarian initiative symbolised by the foundation of the Red Cross led not only to the Geneva Conventions, but also to those signed at The Hague in 1899 and 1907, which dealt with the conduct of hostilities and with limitations on the use of certain weapons. It might even be said that the entire modern effort to secure the peaceful settlement of disputes and the outlawing of war also stems indirectly from the little Geneva Convention of 1864. The Hague Conventions paved the way for our modern commissions of inquiry and arbitration courts. The Covenant of the League of Nations drew its ultimate inspiration from the same humanitarian source, and the Kellogg Pact went so far as to prohibit the recourse to war. In our own day, the Charter of the United Nations reflects the same great tradition.

In a sense, all this was foreseen by one of the founders of the Red Cross, Gustave Moynier, who wrote in 1864: "Now that we have entered on this course, we have taken a decisive step on a slope where there is no stopping; the end of the road cannot be less than the condemnation of war in absolute terms".

The Geneva Conventions

International humanitarian law as it exists today forms part of public international law and consists of a number of legal agreements designed to protect the individual. We may recall the famous phrase of Talleyrand, who declared that international law rests on the "principle that in peace the nations should do as much good to one another, and in war as little harm, as possible."

Humanitarian law falls into two main categories — the international law of war and law relating to human rights. This second category has been proclaimed both by the League of Nations and the United Nations and is a mainspring of the latter's activity, including such manifestations as the Universal Declaration of Human Rights, the International Convention on the Status of Refugees, the repression of slavery and so on. I am not primarily concerned here with this aspect of humanitarian law.

The law of war stems from the notion that warfare does not sever all legal relations between States. Certain principles based both on reason and on humanitarian feeling must still continue to exert their influence over the most violent antagonists. This law of war can again be subdivided into what one might call the law of The Hague and the law of Geneva.

The law of The Hague aims at controlling the conduct of hostilities and the use of arms, following the principle that belligerents do not have unlimited rights concerning the means which they may use to injure the enemy. The law of Geneva, or, as we might call it Red Cross law, is more particularly humanitarian in character, since its purpose is to protect the victims of war and those who are unable to injure others and who therefore call for special care. I would like to devote the rest of my remarks to this Geneva aspect of humanitarian law.

The 1864 Convention has been revised three times since that date. When the First World War drew attention to the need for fresh regulations to protect prisoners of war, a second Geneva Convention for this purpose was concluded in 1929. Preliminary proposals for it had been prepared by the International Committee of the Red Cross (ICRC).

At the same time, the law protecting civilians was seen to be in urgent need of extension. Unfortunately, the ICRC failed in its efforts to establish the status of civilians at the same time as that of prisoners of war. It was not until 1934 that an International Conference of the Red Cross approved a draft Convention for the protection of civilians. International sanction was to have been given to this Convention by a diplomatic conference which was to meet in 1940. I need hardly explain why that action could not be taken.

During the Second World War, the Geneva Conventions then in force gave a striking demonstration of what could be done to aid millions of prisoners. Where they were observed, the death rate among prisoners of war did not exceed the normal level of some 10 per cent, whereas, in concentration camps whose inmates enjoyed no legal protection, mortality was sometimes as high as 90 per cent.

After 1945, the ICRC set about completing the Geneva Conventions in the light of its latest experience, concentrating upon the civilians, whose interests had been so cruelly neglected. Working together with international experts, the ICRC produced draft conventions which were discussed by the diplomatic conference summoned in Geneva by the Swiss Government in April-August 1949. This Conference brought together almost all the nations of the world, but an even more remarkable fact was that no less than 80 States have ratified these basic charters of humanity.

When we come to consider the progress achieved in 1949, we have to remember that the first necessity was to ensure that the Geneva Conventions should not be applicable only after a regular declaration of war, but as soon as hostilities actually break out. For the Red Cross, a war exists once there are wounded and prisoners needing help and therefore the Conventions apply whether or not a state of war is recognised by one of the parties and in all cases of occupation, even if no military resistance is offered.

A still more delicate problem was that of ensuring that the Conventions should apply in civil wars. The victims of such wars, in which personal animosities are particularly bitter, are in urgent need of protection, but the difficulties were considerable. Were States to bind themselves in regard to future adversaries still unknown to them, who were to rebel against their authority, who might be acting in defiance of all law and who might not regard themselves as bound by any legal obligations? The view was expressed that such action might not only encourage rebellion, but also paralyse legally constituted governments even in dealing with acts of banditry.

After months of discussion the Diplomatic Conference adopted in Article 3 what amounts to a miniature Convention in itself. In this Article it is laid down that in hostilities which are not international in character the guiding principle of humanity must, in all circumstances, be observed. This covers the treatment of non-combatants and people taking no further part in the fighting, the banning of torture, the seizure of hostages and irregular sentences or executions. Belligerents were called on to reach separate agreements which would extend further than this basic humanitarian minimum and the ICRC was authorized to offer its services to help belligerents in this respect. A safety-valve for national susceptibilities was provided by the statement that these undertakings would have no effect on the legal status of parties to a given conflict. This Article 3 introduced a revolutionary element into traditional international law and it is under its auspices that the ICRC has been able to carry on humanitarian work in such situations as that resulting from hostilities in Algeria.

One of the most important innovations introduced by the 1929 Convention was that by which "protecting powers" supervise its execution. These powers are neutral States asked to represent the interests of one belligerent in dealings with the other and, in addition, ICRC delegates pay regular visits to prisoner of war camps. The protecting powers did much to improve the lot of prisoners during the Second World War, but the shocking fact remains that some 70 per cent of the prisoners taken in that war were not allowed to benefit from the services of any protecting power, because some States refused to admit ICRC missions and to recognize neutral States as protecting powers.

The 1949 Conference proposed the creation of a new supervisory body in such cases or recourse to an existing organ such as the ICRC. Should there be no protecting power, the State in question would be under an obligation to deal with a substitute.

One result of the Convention of 1949 was to emphasize still further the role of the ICRC in time of war. This body, a private and independent association of Swiss citizens who are co-opted on to it, is thus completely national in membership, and yet, as far as its mission is concerned, international in the highest degree. It is the neutral organ *par excellence* in time of war or civil disturbance. It benefits from the fact that its members are citizens of a small country without political ambitions and traditionally neutral. Thus, during the Second World War, its delegates paid no less than 11,000 visits to prisoner of war camps on both sides. In addition, the ICRC founded and operates the Central Tracing Agency for prisoners of war and civilians, besides taking an active part in the transportation and distribution of supplies.

It will be seen that the essential purpose of the Geneva Conventions is to safeguard the individual's rights. Non-combatants and those no longer fighting must be protected in all circumstances. Enemy troops who lay down their arms must receive the same treatment as those of the national army, without discrimination, and priority in treatment must be given only on medical grounds. In consequence, an area of immunity must be created around the wounded and symbolized by a red cross. This immunity extends to hospitals, ambulances and other vehicles and to the medical personnel who, for their part, must remain above the conflict and observe strict military neutrality. When medical personnel are taken prisoner, they must be repatriated as soon as they are no longer needed to look after other prisoners of war. The second Geneva Convention extended these principles to warfare at sea, while the third Convention provided for humane treatment of prisoners and hygienic standards in POW camps.

One difficult problem before the 1949 Conference concerned the treatment to be accorded to "partisans", such as had played so important a role in various resistance movements during the Second World War. These were considered not as regular combatants, but as *francs-tireurs*, and they could claim no rights on capture by the enemy. It was obvious that the Geneva Convention could not be drawn up so as to protect every individual who commits acts of sabotage or who joins an underground movement against the authorities. A solution was found for this problem by considering organised resistance movements as being in the same category as militia groups and volunteer corps which do not form part of the regular armed forces of a belligerent State but nevertheless look to that State for support and satisfy four conditions necessary for recognition under the international law of war. These are: a) to operate under the orders of a responsible leader, b) always to wear a distinctive emblem recognizable from a distance, c) to bear arms openly and d) to obey the laws and customs of war. It has, of course, to be admitted that these conditions would have excluded the members of most resistance movements in the last war, since secrecy was essential to their operation. In 1949, perhaps the most important question of all was the problem of protecting civilians. In this field, the great step forward was an international agreement that all enemy civilians held captive for any reason will henceforth enjoy a similar status to that of prisoners of war. House arrest or internment are the severest measures to which a State can have recourse against such civilians and then only if the security of that State renders such measures absolutely necessary. The Convention also prescribes that the case of all such civilians shall be reconsidered as speedily as possible by a competent tribunal. If they remain in internment, the tribunal must reconsider their case at least twice a year and its decisions must be notified to the protecting power.

Article 27 defines the principles applicable to the treatment of civilians and guarantees in all circumstances respect for the individual's person, honour, family rights, religious convictions and way of life. A clause proposed by the ICRC, at the request of various women's organizations, specifically protects the honour of women. Extermination, torture, violence and all physical or moral pressure to obtain information are forbidden. Article 33 bans collective punishment and reprisals and affirms that no protected person may be punished for an act which he did not personally commit. Article 34 declares, with striking simplicity, that the taking of hostages is forbidden. This constitutes another innovation in international law and a great humanitarian victory. Article 49 prohibits deportations. One has only to think of the sufferings endured by millions of people forcibly removed from their homes during the last World War to realize the importance of this item.

Recent Developments of International Law

These Conventions will be effective only in so far as they become widely known and the ICRC and the Swiss Government have directed their efforts to secure both their ratification by all States and their wide publication throughout the world. Meanwhile, further extensions of humanitarian law are becoming necessary.

An important problem is that of people imprisoned in their own country as a result of civil disturbances. Such people have often been worse treated by their compatriots than captured enemy troops. By an irony of our time, the ICRC now has to consider the problem of how the humanitarian law of war can be applied to protect the victims of "peace", when no international issues are involved in their ill-treatment. A group of famous international lawyers gave their opinion that the Red Cross could legitimately intervene in this domain and the ICRC has, in fact, already played a humanitarian part in connexion with disturbances in the Americas, Africa and Asia.

We come to what is perhaps the gravest matter of all. The development of weapons of war towards the ultimate in destructive power from carpet bombing through V1's, V2's and napalm bombs to the first hydrogen bombs and beyond has now reached a point where civilization, and even mankind, may be obliterated in another conflict. Certain rules for the conduct of aerial warfare were formulated at The Hague as long ago as 1907 and the world's first aerial bombardment took place not in 1914, but in 1911. Yet, despite the terrifying progress of nuclear physics, governments have taken no action to revise these out-of-date rules. The Red Cross has tried to solve this problem, not by singling out the use of specific weapons, such as atom bombs, but by seeking to set limits to certain forms of modern warfare in general. Many writers claim that the mass bombing of civilians in the Second World War did not really "pay" from the military point of view, although the bombardment of Hamburg caused as many deaths as that of Hiroshima. Moreover, the banning of one weapon might well lead to the invention of another still more terrifying. And at Oradour, the weapon used was a box of matches...

The principle on which the Red Cross is now working is that, irrespective of the weapons used, the civilian population should in no circumstances be exposed to risks out of proportion with the military objective in view. The first step was to call in experts with whose help certain draft rules were prepared. In 1957 these rules were approved in principle at the last International Red Cross Conference, but governments have so far shown no readiness to adopt them.

These suggested rules are designed essentially to protect the civilian population as far as possible from the effects of war. If they were adopted, the only bombardments legally admissible would be those against military objectives as defined in the draft convention, including some in the immediate vicinity of which there are civilian homes. There would also be a ban on the use of all weapons whose harmful effects are liable to get out of hand and extend in space or time, and so constitute a danger to the population. This draft convention is only one of various activities upon which the Red Cross is now engaged. We refuse to be discouraged and, if one method for protecting the civilian population proves ineffective, we shall try others.

It has been the mission of the Red Cross to fight war by endeavoring to humanize it. If the ICRC were to descend into the political arena and argue about the policies of States, the size and nature of their military budgets and so on, it would become involved in insuperable difficulties and would lose its most precious asset, the confidence of both parties to any conflict that may arise. Other organizations are working for peace along political lines and each individual can help them with the means at his disposal, but it is probably true to say that the first Geneva Convention of 1864, modest as it was, enabled the Red Cross to deal one of the heaviest blows ever aimed at the whole concept of war. From that year on the Red Cross flag has been one of the standards raised wherever war has brought its train of suffering to mankind. Its symbol of mercy has won the allegiance of men without reference to race or frontiers, and that allegiance has borne fruit. In the Crimean War, before there was a Red Cross, 60 per cent of the wounded died. In the Korean War, 2 percent of those wounded in the United Nations forces were lost. Are not these figures eloquent?

There can be no doubt that the Red Cross has done much to promote a sense of active solidarity among the peoples of the world and to form a network of moral responsibilities and legal agreements undertaken in common. When war brings its tragic breach in human sympathies, the Red Cross remains as a last gangway between men. In the midst of violence it constantly intervenes, without once using violence. It is perhaps the only great idea in whose name no one has ever been put to death. The Red Cross, like the United Nations, expresses respect for human life and human destiny. Both are a promise of that better world which mankind, working in harmony, could one day achieve.

Date

AF
6